Contents

Twitter Marketing

Promote Yourself and Your Business on Earth's Hottest Social Network

By Steve Weber

Warning and Disclaimer: The information in this book is offered with the understanding that it does not contain legal, financial, or other professional advice. Individuals requiring such services should consult a competent professional.

The author and publisher make no representations about the suitability of the information contained in this book for any purpose. This material is provided "as is" without warranty of any kind.

Although every effort has been made to ensure the accuracy of the contents of this book, errors and omissions can occur. The publisher assumes no responsibility for any damages arising from the use of this book, or alleged to have resulted in connection with this book. This book is not completely comprehensive. Some readers may wish to consult additional books for advice. This book is not authorized or endorsed by Amazon or any other company mentioned in the text.

Published by Stephen W. Weber
Printed in the United States of America
Weber Books www.WeberBooks.com

Author: Steve Weber
Editor: Julie Bird

ISBN: 978-0-9772406-6-1

Also by Steve Weber:

Plug Your Book! Online Book Marketing for Authors

ePublish: Self-Publish fast and profitably for Kindle, CreateSpace, iPhone and Print on Demand

Sell on Amazon: A Guide to Amazon's Marketplace, Seller Central, and Fulfillment by Amazon Programs

The Home-Based Bookstore: Start Your Own Business Selling Used Books

eBay 101: Selling on eBay For Part-time or Full-time Income

Tuning into Twitter

No matter what kind of business you have, its success depends on two things: It must serve a need, and you must find customers.

Most new businesses fail simply because the right people never heard about them. And this is the paradox for entrepreneurs: People aren't paying much attention to traditional marketing and advertising anymore. But free advertising is alive and well. Whatever you want to call it—buzz, word of mouth, peer-to-peer or viral marketing—you can't just manufacture it. You must earn it by engaging your target market.

Fortunately, there is a very straightforward, ethical way of gaining this free exposure: by participating on social networks. And the fastest-growing, easiest-to-learn, most-addictive such network is Twitter

Twitter.com is a free social-networking site, where users submit text-based posts of up to 140 characters called "tweets." These tweets appear instantly on the pages of the user's subscribers (known as "followers"), and also appear on the member's profile page. Tweets can be sent and received through Twitter's Web site, by cellphones using SMS (Short Message Service), or external applications.

Think of it as a cocktail party. You talk to one person, and then move on to someone else. You can eavesdrop without being rude. You can use Twitter to stay in touch with a few friends, or promote your business to the world. You can have a separate account for each purpose. Or you can choose not to directly participate in Twitter at all. In any case, you can use Twitter for what it essentially is: a search engine for discovering what people are talking about right now.

An estimated 6 million people are using Twitter, the most popular site for "microblogging," the practice of communicating with short text messages. Whether your goal is to connect with friends, family, and past acquaintances, or to market yourself, your business, or your products, the possibilities are truly limitless.

This book will explain how to start using Twitter more effectively, for both professional and personal pursuits.

Twitter can provide business owners valuable free exposure to a worldwide pool of new customers and fans. Meanwhile, Twitter serves as a bottomless well of research material for those who care to use it.

Entrepreneurs can no longer depend on interruption-based ads, such as commercials and junk mail, which force consumers to stop what they're doing and pay attention. But with Twitter, you can influence these consumers precisely at the point where they're engaged.

Twitter offers marketers an unprecedented opportunity for marketing because it enables your target market to find you, instead of you finding them. No longer must marketers blast advertisements to people who aren't paying attention.

Twitter already has turned traditional marketing on its head. Forget having to scrape together a huge pile of cash for a marketing campaign, then pray it works. Hundreds of thousands of businesses, large and small, are using Twitter to lure new customers—and talk directly with them—at virtually no cost.

And unlike most traditional advertising, Twitter can pay dividends for years to come because it forges a strong link between you and consumers, enabling your biggest fans to become evangelists for your business. When you're successful, your loyal customers begin spreading the word for you, generating true word of mouth.

In the old days, with postal direct mail or telephone cold-calling, your chance of getting a response from someone who didn't know you was about 2 percent—and that's if you had a big marketing budget and were doing everything right. But today, the social-networking skills described in this book can result in response rates of 80 percent or more.

On Twitter, people opt in to hear your messages. But with this powerful new tool, it's important to learn the ropes because marketing with Twitter is a double-edged sword. Any other member of the community can command a voice as loud as yours. If you earn the community's respect, they'll help spread the word about you better than a million-dollar ad campaign. But if you're boring, you'll be ignored.

Marketing on Twitter is refreshingly simple and pays obvious dividends. You create a profile and lure customers by providing content interesting to them. With the proper effort, any marketing objective can be achieved—to introduce or reinforce your brand image, inspire customer loyalty, or simply drive visitors to your Web site, Internet store, or affiliated retailer.

If your marketing resources are limited, Twitter is a no-brainer. It's much simpler than building and maintaining a Web site. On the other hand, if you already have a Web site, Twitter can be your biggest source of targeted traffic.

The benefits of Twitter

Twitter is a conversation tool. You can start Twitter conversations, you can add to them, or you can read conversations among other tweeters. It's within these conversations that the value of Twitter emerges. Twitter can be exactly what you want it to be: a social tool, a business tool, a promotional tool, a research tool, or a combination of whichever tools you choose.

On the **personal** side with Twitter, you can:

- Stay abreast of current events.
- Keep up with family and friends.
- Meet new friends with similar interests.
- Share news about your life, work, or hobbies.
- Talk about books, movies, TV shows, music, art, or virtually anything else.
- Share opinions.
- Research topics, people, places, and things.

To small business owners: your input is crucial in the health insurance reform debate. Please weigh in: http://bit.ly/Wj3J1
BarackObama
Barack Obama
Getting so many suggestions on titles for my new book. What's the best way to do a survey?
PatBarone
Pat Barone
Aug 6th: Hiroshima Day: NYC Die-In for Peace http://bit.ly/630Mp
yokoono
Yoko Ono
"When I am dead, I hope it may be said: 'His sins were scarlet, but his books were read.'" #quote Hilaire Belloc
WeberBooks
Steve Weber
How to get book publicity from bloggers. (any product publicity actually) http://om.ly/?DrPf
GuyKawasaki
Guy Kawasaki
Toyota is pulling tweets live into their banner ad for the Prius - pretty cool eh? http://twitpic.com/cv14r
chrislindinger
Attention all scrabble players, question, is pigsriot a word
THE_REAL_SHAQ
And down goes a potted plant. You wonder why I call my blog Dirt & Noise.
ilinap
ilinap
Lunch Runs:VERDE-12PM-3PM@Market Lofts-645 W. 9th Street, entrance on Hope St.; ROJA: 12PM-3PM@Best Buy - 11301 W.Pico Blvd
kogibbq

- Share links of interest.
- Follow people you find interesting, such as celebrities, politicians, and musicians.
- Automatically send your tweets to other social networking sites.

Along with the above, the **business** side of Twitter allows you to:

- Create, reinforce, and expand your brand.
- Promote your business, products, and self.
- Expand your audience.
- Network with like-minded business professionals.
- Network with customers, clients or readers.
- Gather opinions on your business or products).
- Find new employees and associates by asking for recommendations.
- Forward traffic to other online destinations.
- Offer networking for employees.
- Find new business prospects.
- Schedule events and meetings.

The Twitter platform gives each user the freedom and ability to derive exactly what they want. Some of the benefits are easier to achieve than others, but none is especially difficult. Add in the many available Twitter applications, and the service becomes even more flexible.

Twitter success stories

The best way to determine how your business can benefit from social networking is to view some examples of what others are doing.

Big companies use Twitter to push their products to people who might be interested. Intuit, which makes budgeting and tax-preparation software, scours Twitter for people mentioning "Mint," a popular personal-finance Web site. Marketing folks at

Intuit then send a message with information about the company's products.

Small local shops are using Twitter too. Bakeries post a tweet when cookies are coming out of the oven, and within minutes, customers are at the door. True Massage & Wellness in San Francisco tweets when its masseuses have open time, and offers discounts for same-day appointments. The spa's owner, Mary Jenn, is able to book each day solid.

For some, Twitter is a free 24-hour consulting service. You can participate in—or initiate—a brainstorming session about virtually anything. For example, on a recent Thursday afternoon, I was stuck trying to think of a title for a forthcoming book. I asked my Twitter followers to suggest more ideas. Within five minutes, I had 10 more titles, most better than the handful I'd struggled with for days.

No matter what their business, companies are using Twitter to gain recognition, higher sales, and awareness of their products and services. For example:

J.R. Cohen, operations manager for Coffee Groundz Café in Houston, credits Twitter with doubling his clientèle. Soon after joining Twitter, Cohen was accepting takeout orders online, just in time for customers zipping through the drive-through.

Jesse McDougall, Web manager for sustainable-living publisher publisher Chelsea Green, has boosted his business with Twitter. Every Wednesday, he runs a simple contest, asking followers to visit the Chelsea Green Web site, choose a book they'd like to win, and then tweet the title. The 10th person who does so wins the book.

Chelsea Green also runs a program called "Ask the Author" on its blog and Twitter. These promotions have boosted traffic at Chelsea Green's Web site and prompted write ups at Huffington Post, Tree Hugger, and other book blogs, bringing exposure to millions of new potential readers.

When US Airways Flight 1549 ditched in the Hudson River in January 2009, the first reports and pictures came from Twitter, scooping the professional news media.

Surgeons in Milwaukee, Wis., tweeted live updates of a knee replacement surgery. Using the free TwitPic photo-sharing service, the Aurora Health Care surgical team provided a running commentary and updates of the procedure.

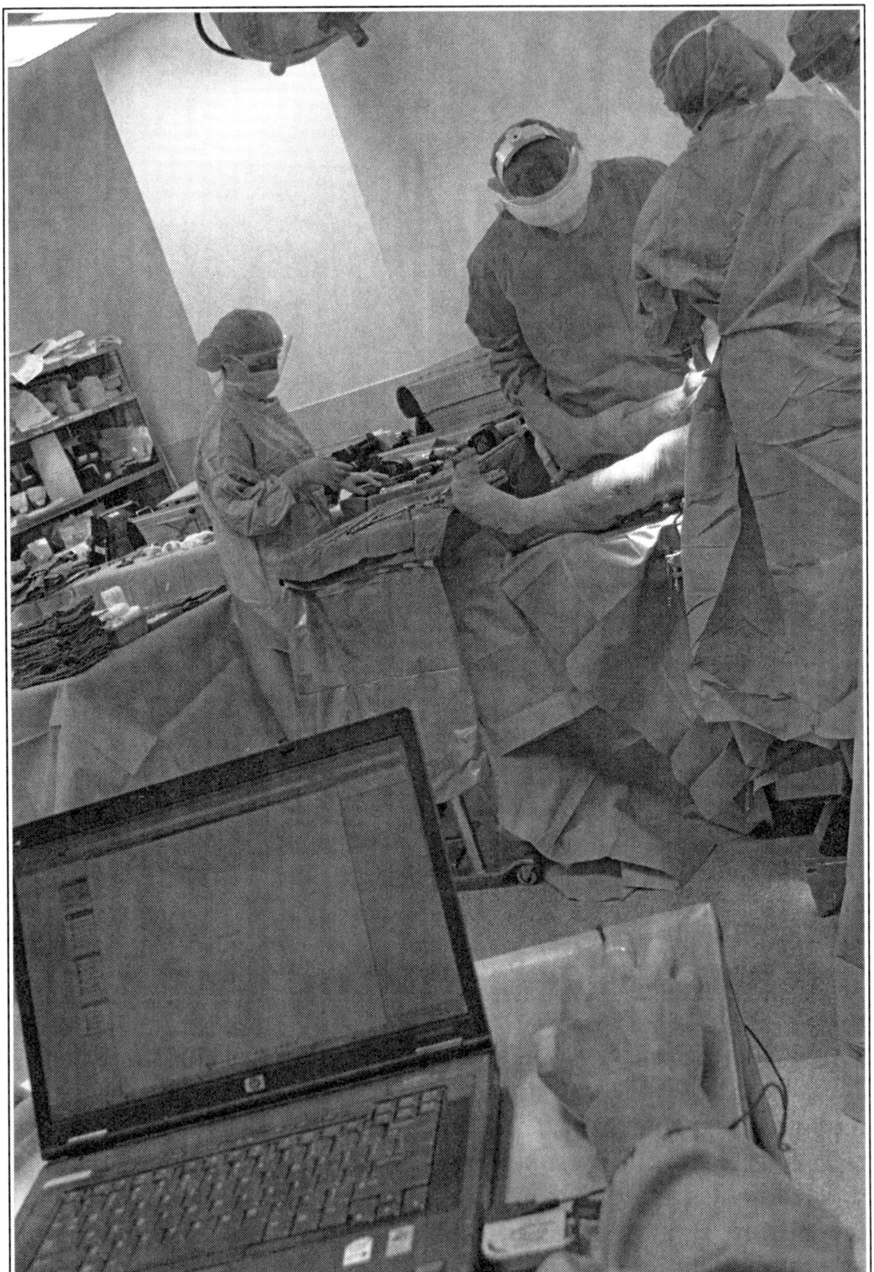

Kogi Korean BBQ, a vendor of Korean barbecue takeout food in Los Angeles, has gained thousands of new customers by tweeting the location of its food trucks. More than 40,000

Twitter users follow the company's updates, which broadcast real-time locations of delivery trucks, as well as "secret" menu items. Even more impressive is the company's loyal customer base, which has created YouTube tributes for the moving restaurant.

Dover Downs Hotel & Casino erected a billboard near Washington, D.C., asking passersby to follow the company's Twitter account. Anyone over the age of 21 who subscribes gets instructions on obtaining free slot play credits at the casino. The resort also sponsors "Tweetups" at a restaurant in the hotel.

Famous folks on Twitter

Who else is on Twitter? It might be more appropriate to ask who *isn't* on Twitter. All sorts of celebrities—from politicians to athletes to musicians, authors to CEOs, and more. Much more. Here's just a small sampling of some of the well-known people who use Twitter. You can visit them by typing into your browser http://twitter.com/ and the usernames given here:

Authors

Deepak Chopra (Deepak_Chopra)
Neil Gaiman (neilhimself)
Tim O'Reilly (timoreilly)
John Scalzi (Scalzi)

Actors

John Cleese (johncleese)
Stephen Fry (stephenfry)
Ashton Kutcher (aplusk)
Demi Moore (mrskutcher)
William Shatner (WilliamShatner)

Business executives

Richard Branson, chairman of Virgin Group (richardbranson)
Steve Case, co-founder of America Online (stevecase)
Richard Jalichandra, CEO of Technorati (jalichandra)
Kevin Rose, founder and CEO of Digg.com (kevinrose)
Mark Zuckerburg, CEO of Facebook (finkd)

Musicians

Coldplay (coldplay)
Neil Diamond (NeilDiamond)
Jay-Z (S_C_)
John Mayer (johncmayer)
MC Hammer (MCHammer)

Politicians

President Barack Obama (BarackObama)
Vice President Joe Biden (joebiden)
Newt Gingrich (newtgingrich)
Sen. John McCain (SenJohnMcCain)
Gov. Arnold Schwarzenegger (schwarzenegger)

Roots of Internet social networking

The roots of Internet social networking can be traced back to 1985, with "The Well," a popular electronic bulletin board. For the first time, members of an online community could communicate 24 hours a day, seven days a week, without any "real life" contact. Today, The Well has been supplanted by newer online communities, where participants can post articles, view pictures, share their opinions, promote themselves and their businesses, and conduct research. Many of the sites are free or low-cost, and the possibilities are endless.

Facebook (http://facebook.com)

Facebook is a free Web site that allows users to associate with other members connected by a city, school, region, employer, or by interests and hobbies. Facebook was originally limited to college students, but now is open to virtually anyone with Internet access.

MySpace (http://myspace.com)

MySpace is another free Web site where users can create profiles, post blogs, share music, videos, and photos. Members can connect with friends, co-workers, family, and anyone else.

LinkedIn (http://linkedin.com)

LinkedIn is the most popular networking site focusing exclusively on business use. With an interconnected worldwide network of professionals, the site encompasses 170 industries and 200 countries.

In addition to accounts at these sites, you can have your own Web site or blog, too. Think of it as a virtual, and public, journal where anyone can express their opinion, share pictures and videos, give reviews, promote their businesses and products, and interact with their readers.

Internet social networking gives any person, anywhere in the world, the ability to connect with millions of people at any time of the day or night.

Finding your audience is another story.

How to use this book

The beginning of this book outlines the basics of Twitter, and debunks several Twitter myths. Then we'll cover signing up for Twitter, what to think about before you tweet, how to create your profile page, and how to gain followers.

The middle section of the book focuses on effective tweeting, marketing your business, and personalizing Twitter. We'll explore legal issues—defamation, privacy and negligence—so you can protect yourself from the very beginning. Finally, we look at what the future might hold for Twitter.

While reading this book, try to clarify these main ideas:

- Your purpose for using Twitter.
- The results you'd like to see.
- How much time you have to devote to Twitter.
- What type of audience you hope to gain.

Getting started with Twitter is extraordinarily simple, but the time you spend thumbing through this book might save you untold trouble and confusion.

Please send me a tweet and let me know what you think of this book and Twitter.

— Steve Weber
— http://twitter.com/WeberBooks

Before you tweet

At this point, you might be eager to start tweeting. Do yourself a favor first, though, and think about Twitter in the same way you think about purchasing an item that requires assembly.

Imagine that you just arrived home with a big cardboard box of something that is in pieces and parts, and you need to make it whole. Are you the type of person who will read through the instructions first, then methodically piece the object together? Or would you rip the box open and jump in?

Twitter is easy to sign up for. It's even easy to begin using. But if you jump in too quickly, you might find yourself wishing you'd taken some time to plan.

If your plan is 100 percent social, you'll likely cruise ahead without too many issues. On the other hand, those with more business-minded Twitter plans will want to consider each stage before moving on.

Define your Twitter purpose

Why are you joining Twitter? You should have a clear idea, and it should be more than "everyone else is doing it, so I will too." Do you want to:

- Chat with knowledgeable people about a niche subject?
- Keep up to date on current events?
- Keep up to date with family and friends?

- Learn more about a topic of interest, either business or social?
- Promote yourself, your business, a product or service?
- Drive traffic to other online personae or identities?
- Create, retain, or increase your personal or professional brand?
- Gather feedback about your projects?
- Network with others with similar interests?
- Network with clients and customers?
- Offer customer support or feedback?
- Gather and offer opinions on things like current events, books, movies, or restaurants?
- Have fun and meet new people?

We're scratching the surface of what's possible with Twitter; these are the starting points.

If you're considering using Twitter for your business, including promotion, branding, networking, researching, gaining feedback, or even to give your employees a place to touch base throughout the day, you'll want to consider these questions:

- How many days per week are you willing to devote to Twitter?
- How much time per day do you want to devote to Twitter?
- Will you want to use Twitter for social reasons, as well? If so, strongly consider using two different Twitter accounts to distinguish between business and social.
- Who are you? How do you talk? More to the point, how should the voice of your company sound to your followers? Funny? Serious? Practical? Informative? All of the above, depending on the situation?
- Are you able to maintain consistency?

Thinking of the exact purposes for which you plan to use Twitter will help you create specific strategies to meet each goal. Consider the best type of strategy for your particular business, with an aim toward drawing interest. What would work best? News alerts,? Sharing stats? Offering deals or holding contests?

Do you mainly want to broadcast messages, or participate in conversations? Think about your company and your brand, and then ... think outside the box.

Your Twitter identity

Selecting the correct Twitter name is essential. Because Twitter is so simple, Twitter names are more important than on other social networks. Although it's possible to change your Twitter name later, it's better to get it right the first time. People will associate your name with your brand and image. Changing it later can confuse and alienate your followers.

Here are the ground rules:

- Length matters. Keep your name short and sweet. The longer the name, the more of the 140-character limit your name will consume with each tweet.
- Names can include letters, numbers, and underscores (although they're hard for some people to type, and not recommended).
- You can't use "twitter" in your name.
- Avoid numbers unless they're part of your business identity.
- Names can include uppercase and lowercase letters, and can make a Twitter name more legible. For example, JohnBrown is easier to read than JOHNBROWN or johnbrown.
- Your Twitter username will also be used in your Twitter Web address.

So, what name is right for you? It depends partly on how you plan to use Twitter, and the identity you want to promote.

- If you're using Twitter mainly for personal reasons, try to use your real name (unless you want to be anonymous). Folks who already know you will have an easier time finding you.
- For a personal or social account, don't use your business name, the name of your employer, or anything else related to your work. If it's social, keep it social.

- For a business account, it's critical to use a name representative of your company. Again, this will make it easier for people to find you, and therefore, to follow you.
- If you're creating a business account, but are well-known by your personal name, then your personal name is fine. However, if you also want to create a social Twitter account, make sure the two names are distinct enough to prevent confusion. You might use a nickname, hobby, or some other type of identifying name for your social account that only those close to you would know.
- If you or your business already have a well-known virtual identity on other social networking sites, consider using the same name for Twitter.

Is your name taken yet?

Checking to see if a name is available is easy. You can type it in on the sign-up page (https://twitter.com/signup) and see if it is available before you even sign up . It's a good idea to create a list of possibilities and then see what is available. If you have a name you want to protect, it's worth signing up now so it's not snagged first by someone else.

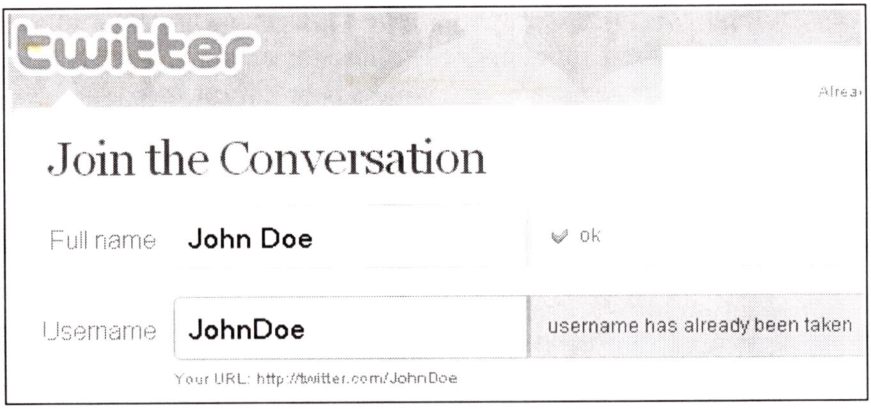

If, for whatever reason, you decide you've signed up with the wrong name, you can change it later. Click on the "settings" link in the top right corner of your Twitter page. On the Settings page, you have the option of changing your username at any time. You'll retain all your current followers, although you will want to notify them about the change.

Before you change your username, consider:

- Your name is your brand. People might be confused and new followers might have trouble finding you after the change.
- Because your username will also be your Web address on Twitter, changing it will break any links from other Web sites.
- If your profile is set to "public," Google might index some of your messages with links to the message. Obviously, changing your username would break those links as well.

You'll also want to consider other names you might want to reserve, even if you don't plan on using them immediately. If you own several different domain names, for example, you might want to register those names on Twitter. That way, you won't have to worry that someone else will appropriate them, and possibly misrepresent your brand.

If you have a common name, it's probably no longer available on Twitter. What if your real name, product name, or business name are already taken? Do you have any recourse? Well, yes and no. It all depends on the situation and the name itself.

Naming issues on Twitter

What if someone is using your business name or something you've trademarked as their Twitter name? Like Internet domain names in general, Twitter names are assigned on a first-come, first-serve basis. But Twitter names aren't necessarily "owned" by whoever registered the name first. If it receives a complaint, Twitter can revoke the name assigned to any account, for any reason.

If someone else is using your personal name, you really don't have any options unless you're a celebrity. In that case, your personal name is also your brand, and Twitter often will intervene in such cases. For example, when rapper Kanye West tried to register his name on Twitter and discovered it was already in use by an impostor, Twitter reassigned the name.

If you're not well-known and your real name is already taken, your best option might be an abbreviation or variation on your name. If, for example, someone named John Thomas Baker discovers that the name JohnBaker is already taken, he could try for:

- JBaker
- BakerJ
- JTBaker
- JTB
- JTB
- JTomBaker

If none of those combinations works, then John Baker has a little thinking to do. If he's a sports fanatic, and loves soccer, he could combine the word "sports" or "soccer" with his initials. Perhaps he could add the name of his city or state. With a little creativity, most people are able to find a Twitter name that works for them.

Trademarked names:

If someone is using a name of your business or trademark, you have more leverage. This is known as "name squatting" and is against Twitter's rules. To report a case, send a tweet to Twitter's spam address, such as this: "@spam the @JohnDoe profile is a squatter." Be sure to include the word "squatter" in your tweet so Twitter's staff will find it.

Selling usernames is against Twitter rules. So if someone has tried to sell you a Twitter username, report it.

Unfortunately, even if Twitter does decide to reassign the name, it might insist on keeping it out of use for several months.

If alerting Twitter doesn't get you the desired results, your last resort is to take the case to federal court. In some cases, squatters willingly stop using a name to avoid legal fees.

Book titles:

If you're an author who wants to tweet under the title of your book, and someone else is already using it, you'll want to determine why. Are they a fan? Are they another author who also has a book with the same title?

In the case of another author, there probably isn't a lot you can do. Instead of tweeting under your title name, what about the name of a character or topic?

If the username belongs to a fan, enter into a conversation with them. They'll probably be thrilled to hear from you. You might even find them willing to give up the name. If they're not willing, however, feel free to send the "squatter" tweet to Twitter.

Negative issues can arise from name squatting, such as defamation and fraud. If you suspect defamation or fraud by someone using your name, contact Twitter, and perhaps an attorney.

The best defense is a strong offense. Even if you're not ready to begin using Twitter today, if the name you want is available, snag it fast.

Exploring Twitter truths and myths

Twitter is something of a craze, yet is vastly misunderstood. Some try Twitter for a short time, only to walk away confused. Others resist joining Twitter, based on myths and misconceptions. Let's face it, people either understand Twitter, or they don't.

Many of those who try Twitter become hooked, but a sizable portion just don't "get it. " The crowd that doesn't get it has usually fallen for some myth or misunderstanding about Twitter, such as:

- Twitter is annoying.
- Twitter is a time-waster,
- Twitter is shallow.
- Twitter is rude.
- Twitter's 140-character limit isn't worth the effort.
- Twitter forces you to follow anyone who follows you.

Perhaps there's a nugget of truth here and there. But the bigger truth is that it's up to you—and other users—to decide how Twitter functions in your lives. What you get out of Twitter depends mostly on what you put into it.

Twitter is a time-waster

- One of the biggest complaints about Twitter is that it is nothing more than groups of people talking about trivial parts of their day. And sure, there are those who love to share what they ate for breakfast, lunch, and dinner seven days a week. If there's too much "noise" on your Twitter account, you can simply quit following those folks. Choose your interests, find the people who share them, and follow them instead.

Twitter is shallow

- This is based on the idea that Twitter is nothing more than an expression of narcissism, and that tweeters just like to hear themselves tweet. Or, more accurately, see themselves tweet. If that's not your thing, you'll find plenty of tweeters who spend their Twitter time conversing about a lot of subjects other than themselves.

Twitter is rude

- Many people who haven't fully discovered Twitter mistakenly believe they must read every word someone tweets, and then answer—or be considered rude. That's just not the case. Twitterers don't expect all of their tweets will be read by all of their followers all of the time. Everyone is ignored part of the time.

Twitter's limit of 140 characters is too confining

- Twitter is a microblogging service, and as such, it limits the length of tweets to 140 characters. Can you say anything useful in such a short space? Of course you can. When you're forced to be brief, you get to the point.

Twitter will pair you with friends you don't like

- Twitter doesn't force you to follow anyone, whether they're following you or not. Whether you decide to follow all of your followers, some of your followers, or even none of your followers, is up to you.

These myths are held mostly by folks who haven't yet tried Twitter—or perhaps tried it briefly and stopped. For most people, it takes a week or two before they realize the benefits of Twitter.

But what separates the successful tweeters from the unsuccessful? Three key ingredients make Twitter the powerhouse that it is, aside from the fun factor and the sheer number of users:

- Simplicity
- Brevity
- Immediacy

Register at Twitter

Registering for Twitter is easy. The sign-up process is simple, and Twitter's "help" section can resolve most questions you might have. Here's how to get started:

1. Go to www.Twitter.com

Once the page loads, the following screen will appear:

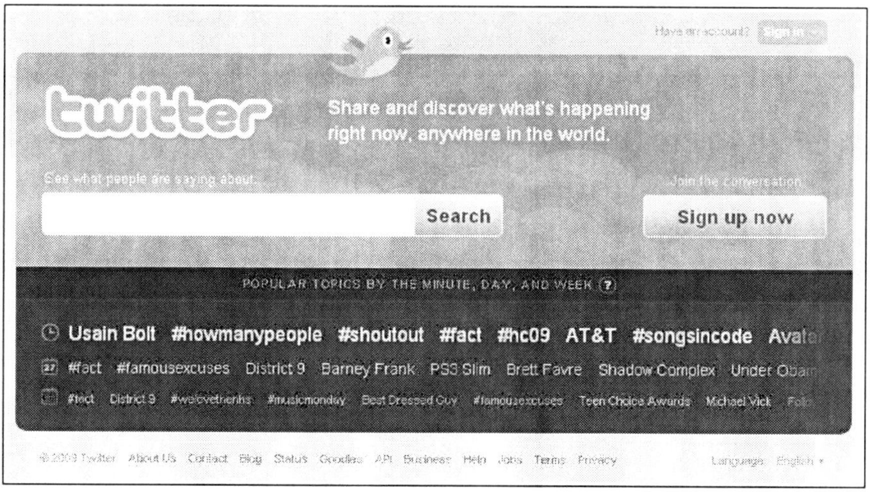

2. Click the "Sign Up Now" button

This page will appear:

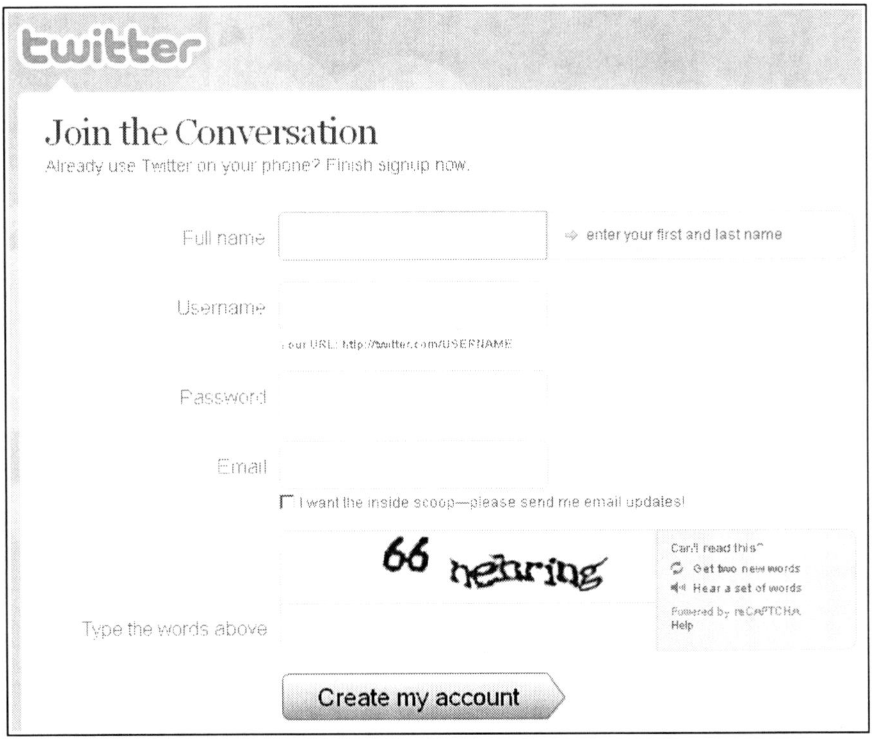

3. Fill in the requested information

- Enter your full name.
- Enter your username (the name you want to be known by on Twitter).
- As soon as you enter a username, the system will search and let you know if the name is available. If it is, move on to the next step. If it isn't, try a different username.
- Enter a password.
- Enter an e-mail address.
- Choose the e-mail address you want associated with this Twitter account.
- Click the box below your e-mail address if you want Twitter to e-mail announcements and alerts to you. Leave it unchecked if you don't.
- Enter in the Captcha Code, those odd-looking words meant to discourage spammers.

- Click "Create my Account."

4. Finding friends—or not

Now that you've registered, Twitter wants to help you find other people you know who also are on Twitter. You'll see this page:

While this is a terrific feature, and one you'll use later, you might want to click the "Skip this Step" link right below the green "Continue" button. That way, you'll have time to refine your settings, design your profile, and add a picture before being flooded with tweets. After you click "Skip this Step," the following page will appear. This is your home page on Twitter, albeit incomplete. There isn't a picture, and the background is the Twitter default. Until you fill in some personal and professional details, no one will know anything about you or your business.

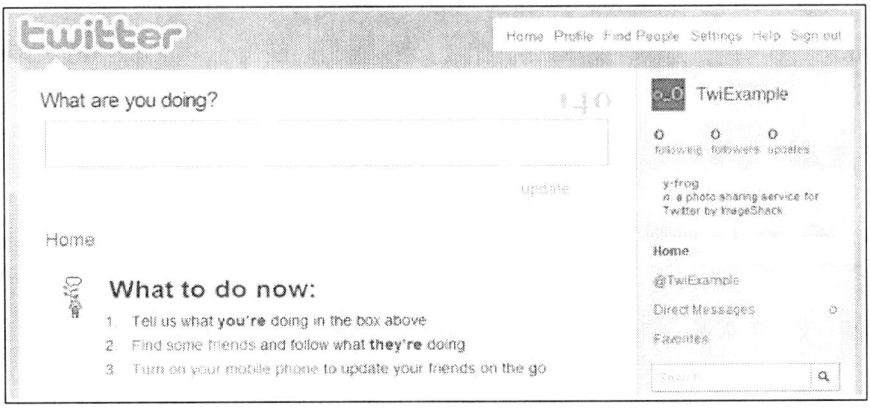

Personalize your Twitter account

Along the top of your Twitter home page, you'll find a menu bar with the following links:

- Home
- Profile
- Find People
- Settings
- Help
- Sign Out

This menu is only available when you're signed in to Twitter. The "Home" and "Profile" links will take you to those respective pages. The "Find People" link will help you locate followers and friends. The "Settings" link is where all the basics for personalizing your Twitter account can be found. The "Help" link leads to an array of questions and answers regarding Twitter. And the "Sign Out" link will log you out of Twitter.

Twitter settings

Now that you've registered, your next objective is to create an identity.

1. Settings

Click on the “Settings” link at the top of the page. The Settings menu offers you six choices:

- Account
- Password
- Devices
- Notices
- Picture
- Design

Clicking on “Settings” will automatically take you to the Account page:

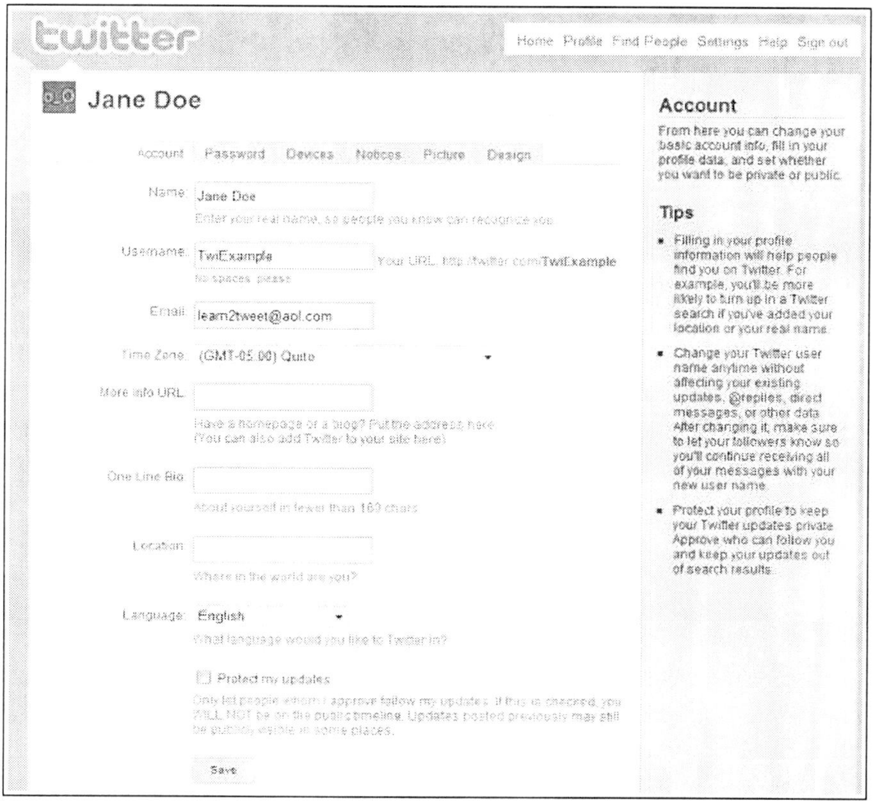

As you can see, the real name, the username, and the e-mail address are already filled in. Your job is to fill in the rest of the information on your account page:

- Scroll to select your time zone. Type in whichever URL you most want the public to see. This could be your Web site, blog, or even another social networking site.
- Type in a mini-bio about you, your company, and your product. You only have 160 characters, so be succinct. Instead of looking at the length as a limitation, see it as a great way to pique interest so visitors will click on your URL to learn more about you. If you're stuck, here are a few tips:

  — Write who you are and what you do.

  — Try to use the same tone you expect to use in your tweets. Meaning, if you plan to be funny (or serious) in your tweets, be funny (or serious) here.

  — Provide at least one interesting, unique detail about yourself, your company, or your product.

- Scroll to select your language.
- Choose whether you want to protect your updates. If so, check the box. If not, leave it unchecked.

In most circumstances, you'll want to have your updates remain "public," especially if you're using Twitter to drum up business. If new people can't read your updates, you won't reach anyone new.

When all of the information on this page is filled in, click on the "Save" link at the bottom of the page.

2. Password

Click on the "Password" link at the top of the Settings page. This page will appear:

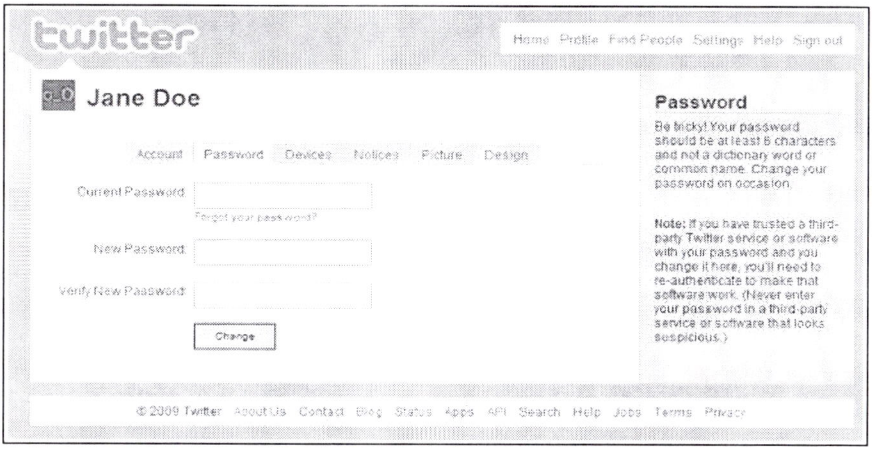

On the password page, you can change your password whenever you'd like. Just fill in the appropriate information and then click "Change."

3. Devices

Click on the "Devices" link at the top of the Settings page. You'll be greeted with this page:

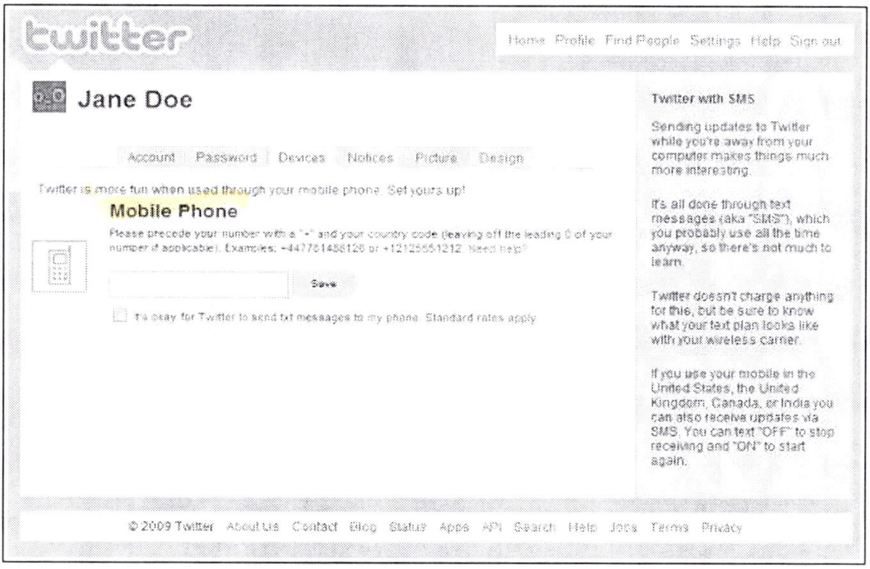

Twitter can be used through your computer or a mobile device. If you'd like to use your phone for Twitter, enter the appropriate information on the devices page. You don't have to make this decision immediately, though. This page is always accessible, and you can add a mobile device at any time. If, however, you only want to use Twitter through your phone, then be sure to input your cell number.

You'll find additional information about using Twitter on a mobile device later in this book, so if you're unsure, leave this page blank for now.

4. Notices

Click on the "Notices" link at the top of the Settings page. The following page will appear:

Here you can control how often you receive notifications from Twitter. The choices:

- **Auto Nudge:** If you haven't posted an update in 24 hours, Twitter will send you a reminder. If you want this reminder, click the box. Otherwise, leave it empty.
- **New Follower E-mails:** Select if you want to be alerted when someone new begins following you. While you can

always see who's following you on Twitter.com, these e-mail alerts are a great way to stay updated.

- **Direct Text E-mails:** Select if you want to receive e-mail alerts when you receive a new direct message. Otherwise, you can view these messages directly through Twitter's Web site.
- **E-mail Newsletter:** Select if you want Twitter to e-mail its newsletter to you. These updates are useful for new users, and you can unsubscribe any time.

When you're finished, click the "Save" button at the bottom of the screen.

5. Picture

Click the "Picture" link at the top of the Settings page. Adding a main picture (also known as an avatar) to your Twitter account is important, as you are putting a face to your username. People connect with faces far more than with text, so don't skip this step. When the page loads, you'll see:

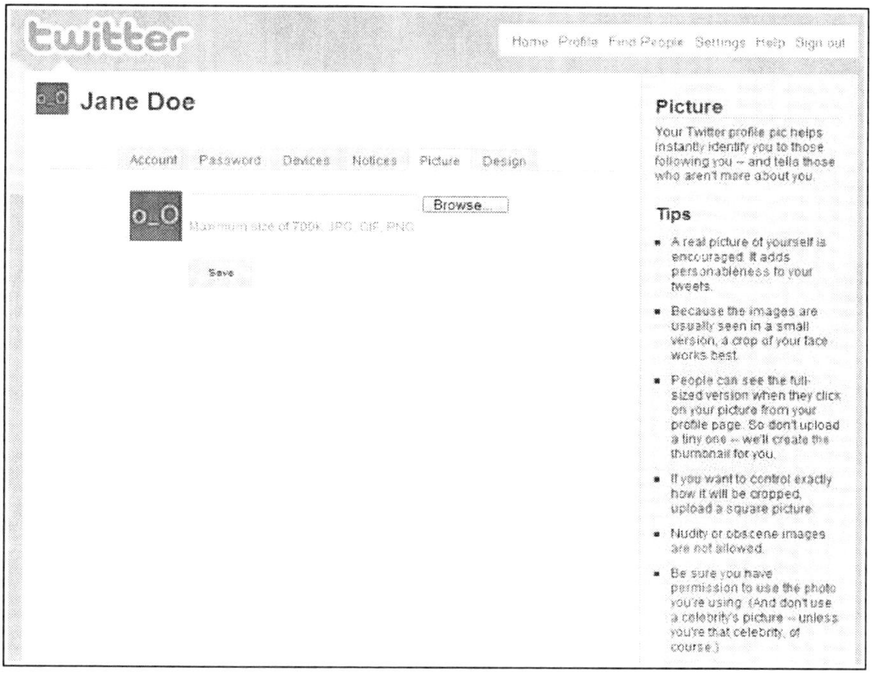

It looks simple, right? Deciding which picture to add might not be as easy. And while it might be tempting to forgo posting a picture, don't give into the temptation. Take a look at the default Twitter image above. It's ugly. Really, really ugly. This is not the photo you want representing you or your business.

So, what type of photo should you use?

- A photo of yourself—a head shot—is often best. People like to know who they're conversing with, and they like to have an image in their head of what that person looks like. This is true even for business tweeters.
- If you really don't want to use a photo of yourself, then choose a picture that reflects some aspect of your personality —perhaps your company logo, a well-known product image, or for authors, your book cover.
- As an alternative to using your company's logo as your avatar, consider using the logo for your Twitter background image. That way, folks can identify with you, but you still have the marketing benefits for your company.

OK, let's assume you're using a headshot as your Twitter avatar. What types of pictures work best?

- A real picture of yourself is encouraged. It adds personableness to your tweets.
- Because the images are usually seen in a small version, a close crop of your face works best—perhaps just enough to show your eyes and smile. If you want to control exactly how it will be cropped, upload a square picture.
- People can see a larger version of your avatar when they click on the image on your profile page. So don't upload a tiny thumbnail, or people who click on your picture won't see a clear image.
- Nudity or "obscene" images are against the rules.
- Be sure you have permission to use the photo you're using. And don't use a photo of someone else—especially of a celebrity.

Once you've selected your avatar photo, adding it to your profile is a snap. Click on "Browse," find the file's location, select it, and click "Open." When Twitter is finished uploading the photo, you'll see it on the page. Click "Save."

6. Design

Click on the "Design" link at the top of the settings page. This page will appear:

Here you can select a "generic" background for your profile. (In the next chapter, we'll explore customized backgrounds, but for now, one of Twitter's cookie-cutter designs will work fine.)

First, decide which of these basic backgrounds appeals to you the most. You can tweak the design colors by clicking "Change Design Colors." When you do, you'll see this page:

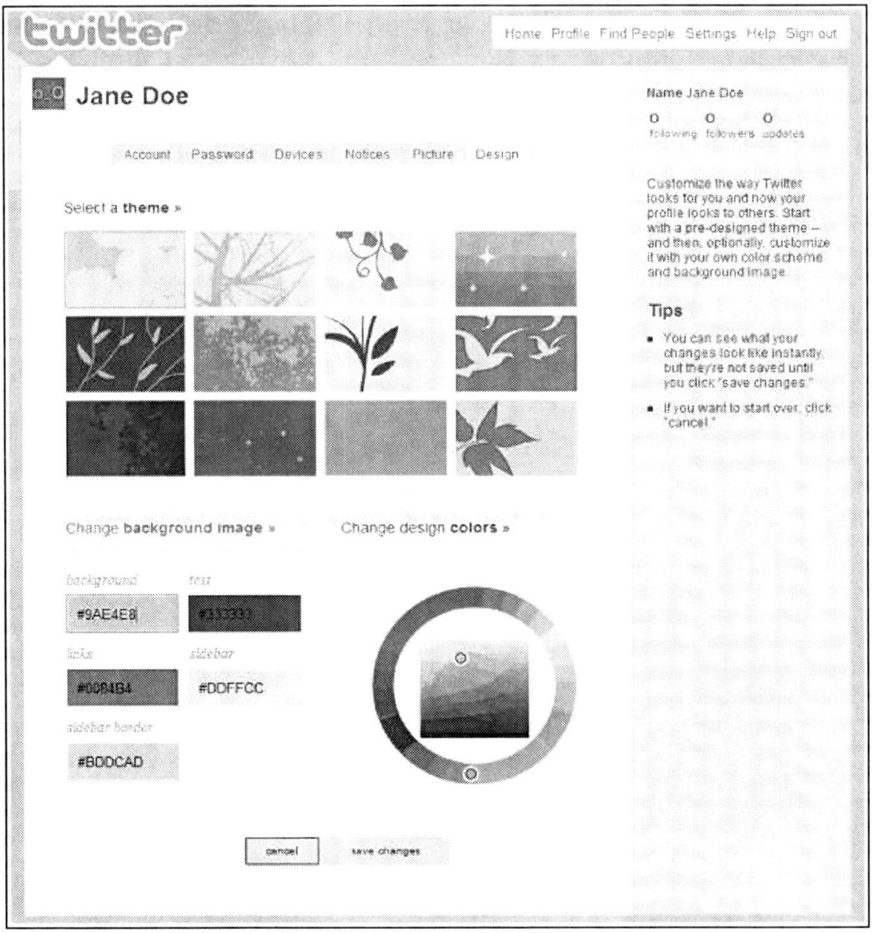

Here, you'll see five colored boxes that make up the background you selected:

- Background
- Text
- Links
- Sidebar
- Sidebar Border

Alongside these boxes is a color wheel, which allows you to customize the design. Click into whichever box you want to alter, and then move the circle within the color wheel until you find the desired hue. Repeat with the remaining boxes, and when you're happy with your new color scheme, click "Save Changes."

Your basic background is now complete. By clicking on the "Profile" link in the upper right-hand corner, you can see how everything came together—your personal information, photo, and the background. If you don't like how something looks, just repeat the steps until you're content with your profile.

Pucker up and tweet!

You're ready. You've registered, chosen and uploaded a photo, written your bio, set your background, and fine-tuned your profile. You're ready to tweet!

Remember, Twitter's primary function is networking. Unlike some other social-networking sites, you cannot be successful in Twitter if you jump in, then tweet only once a week. You don't need to spend an hour a day. But if you're going to build a network, you'll need to spend at least *some* time three or four times a week.

Later on, we'll learn about numerous Twitter add-ons you can use to save time and filter information. But for now, we must start at the beginning.

Tweet first, follow later

Before you begin following anyone, you should send a few tweets just to warm up. When you begin to follow someone, they'll receive a message alerting them. If you don't have any tweets for them to read, they might not find a reason to follow you back. Give them a reason to be interested.

Tweeting will give folks an idea of who you are and what type of value you're going to provide. Start with a minimum of six tweets to take up a decent-sized portion of the white Twitter screen. If you're unsure of what to tweet, here are some suggestions:

- Introduce yourself. Go for a conversational, witty tone.

- Share something you've found of interest lately. This could be a link to a cool YouTube video, an article, a picture, a review for a book you just read, or anything that strikes your fancy.
- Introduce your company or your product (but only after introducing yourself as an individual).
- Greet the Twitter world.
- State you're new to Twitter and would love some advice. You can ask about a particular application, request recommendations on Twitterers who would be interesting to follow based on your business, interests and hobbies, or any other Twitter question you have.
- Your favorite quote(s).
- If you're known for your humor, you can post a funny anecdote, a joke, or anything else in good taste designed to make people laugh. Briefly, of course.
- If you have a blog, you can send out a tweet directing folks to a post you wrote elsewhere.
- Questions are good starting points in real-life conversation, and they work well within Twitter. So ask a few.

Twitter etiquette

With these first tweets, you're sharing a bit of who you are, and giving a taste of what's to come. Have fun with it. But as with any polite conversation, there are a few areas you'll want to avoid:

- Don't overload your Tweets with self-promotion. No more than 10 percent of your tweets should be self-serving. You don't want to come off as a spammer, especially now.
- Do not focus every tweet on your business or product. Again, people want to connect with real people.

- Don't get bogged down in the minutiae of daily life. Your mother might care to know what you ate for breakfast, but nobody else will. Details are good; tedium is bad.
- For business accounts, stay away from polarizing discussions of politics, sex, religion, or morality—unless they pertain to your work, and are what your audience expects. Otherwise, avoid touchy subjects and don't risk alienating many potential new friends.

When you're ready to send that first tweet, just type it in the text box on your Twitter home page and click "Update." You've just made your first tweet. Twitter is fun, even when used for business and marketing purposes, so don't think too hard about these early tweets. Really, all you're doing is creating some basic data for others to view, and hopefully, respond to.

OK, you've banged out a batch of tweets. Now what? Depending on what you twittered about, you might find conversations already beginning. You might even grab a couple of followers right away, which is great. But if you don't, there's nothing to worry about. Your next step is also the first step to gathering an audience, and that is becoming a follower yourself.

Who to follow?

The mechanics of following someone on Twitter are as simple as clicking the "Follow" button below their avatar. But who, exactly, should you follow? It depends on your reason for using Twitter. Among the possibilities:

People you already know

You communicate with these people in some form or fashion already, or have in the past.

- **Your social group.** This includes family, friends, and neighbors, an obvious choice for social Twitterers.

- **Your work peers.** This includes your boss, co-workers, and employees.
- **Past or current schoolmates.** Twitter is a great way to reconnect with your best friend from high school or your roommate from college.
- **Members of clubs and organizations you belong to.** Are you a member of a local writing group? The Chamber of Commerce? Consider your organizations and whether there are folks you'd like to tweet with.
- **Clients, customers, and consumers.** You're already doing business with these people. Here's another way to stay in touch.
- **Providers.** These people provide services, products, or information you've found valuable.

People you want to know

- **Famous folks.** There are a ton of well-known people on Twitter, including celebrities, politicians, musicians, actors, and authors, and many are fun to follow.
- **Smart people.** This group of people is wide and varied, depending on your interests. These are the experts in your field who have interesting things to say and use Twitter as a forum.
- **People like you.** Maybe they work in your industry, maybe they share the same enthusiasm on a topic, or maybe they live in your area. Regardless, there is at least one common denominator between you, so chances are their Twitter connections would interest you.
- **Business prospects.** These are the folks who might be interested in your services or your products.

The great thing about all of these groups is that they have already developed their own connections on Twitter. Join them, and you expand your network, and the power of your voice.

Now that you have an idea what type of people you want to follow on Twitter, how do you actually find them? Fortunately, Twitter has made this very easy.

Become a follower

Twitter has several options for finding people you want to follow. Later, we'll explore third-party services you can use to broaden your search, view rankings, and see a person's rate of activity—even to auto-follow people based on keywords in their profiles or tweets. For now, we'll stick with the basics.

Log in to Twitter, and click the "Find People" link in the upper right-hand menu bar.

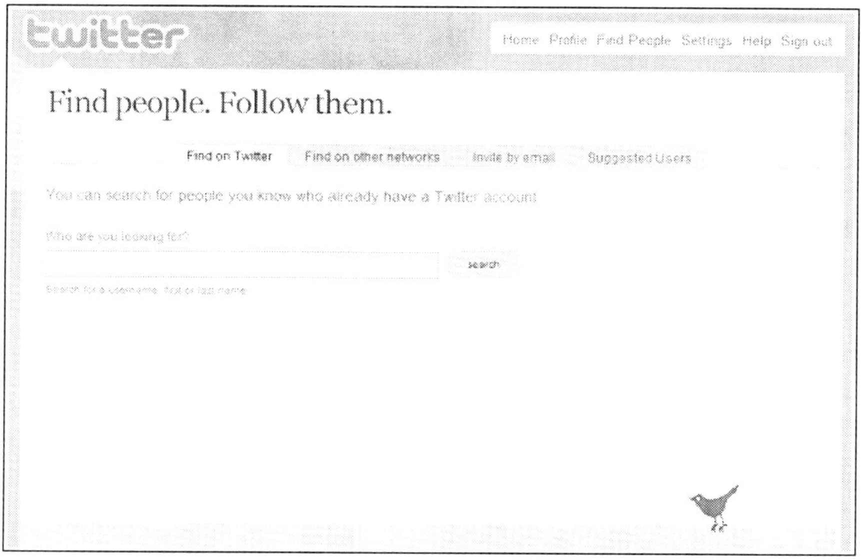

Once the page appears, you're presented with four ways of searching for people:

1) Find on Twitter

The "Find on Twitter" page lets you search Twitter users by usernames and real names. Simply type in the username or the real name of the person you're hoping to find, then click "search." In the results, you'll see the matching profiles, along with their avatars and bios. The ones at the top will have the most followers, like this:

2) Find on other networks

The "Find on other networks" page allows you to search for Twitter uses you already know, based on their e-mail address. This feature works only if you have Web-based e-mail such as GMail, Yahoo, AOL, Hotmail, or MSN. It's a terrific way to see whether the people you know are already on Twitter.

Just click the appropriate e-mail account, type in your e-mail address and your password, and then click "Continue."

Then, you'll see a page displaying which of your contacts are on Twitter (or a message that none of your contacts could be found on Twitter). From here, it's easy to scroll through each person and choose who you want to follow. If you want to follow everyone, simply check the "Select All" box. Click on the "Continue" button and in a few seconds; you'll be following everyone you selected.

3) Invite by e-mail

What if you want to invite people you already know, but who aren't on Twitter yet? Twitter has that taken care of that, too. This page allows you to type in as many e-mail addresses as you like, separated by commas. When you click the "Invite" button, all of the addresses you've typed in will receive an invitation to join you.

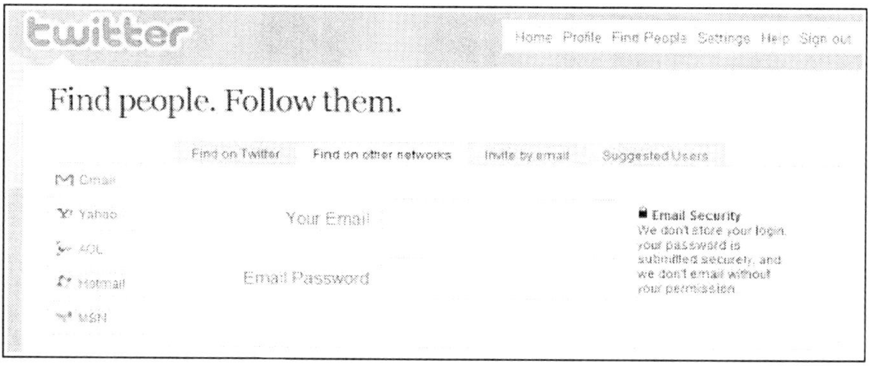

4) Suggested users

The fourth option Twitter offers through its "Find People" tab is the Suggested Users page, compiling a selection of well-known and well-followed Twitterers. Scroll through the list, see if anyone interests you, select them, and when ready, just click "Follow."

While that wraps up Twitter's "find people" options, there is still one more search you can do through Twitter for people, places, subjects, and more. On the home page's right column is a search box, highlighted with an icon of a magnifying glass.

Here, you can type in a subject, place, person, or thing and Twitter will search and pull out any tweets that contain your search criteria. This is a great way to find additional people to follow.

Another way to access Twitter's search is to click the "Search" link found on the bottom margin of both pages. When you click on "Search," this page will appear:

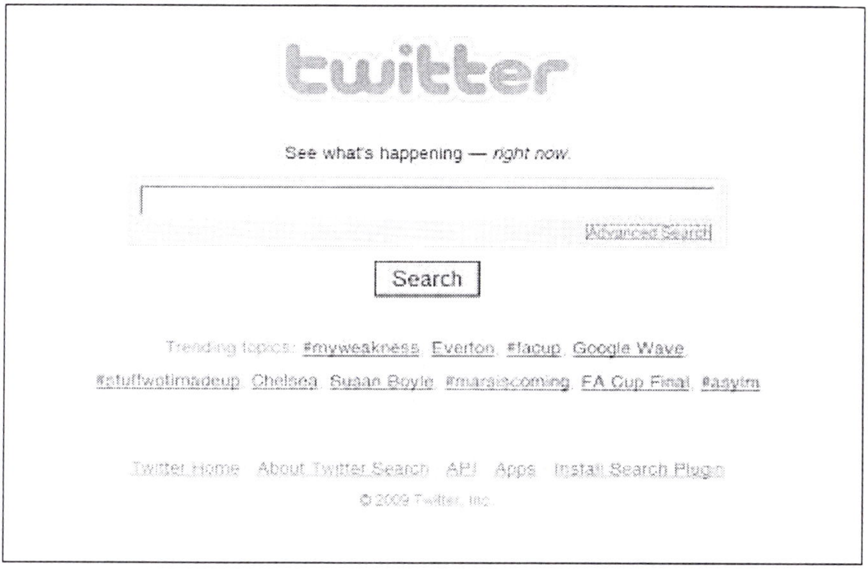

You can take this one step further and refine your search by clicking on the "Advanced Search" link directly below the search box. The Advanced Search form is fairly self-explanatory. You can find tweets that have certain words in them, by who sent them, by who they were sent to, by date, by location, if they contained links, and more. This form will sort through all tweets and pull out the information you're looking for, but with more focused results than the basic search. This is also a great tool for research. Want to know more about an event? Look it up and see what people are saying about it.

While Twitter's options will give you plenty of avenues to find people to follow, many third-party applications can be of great use.

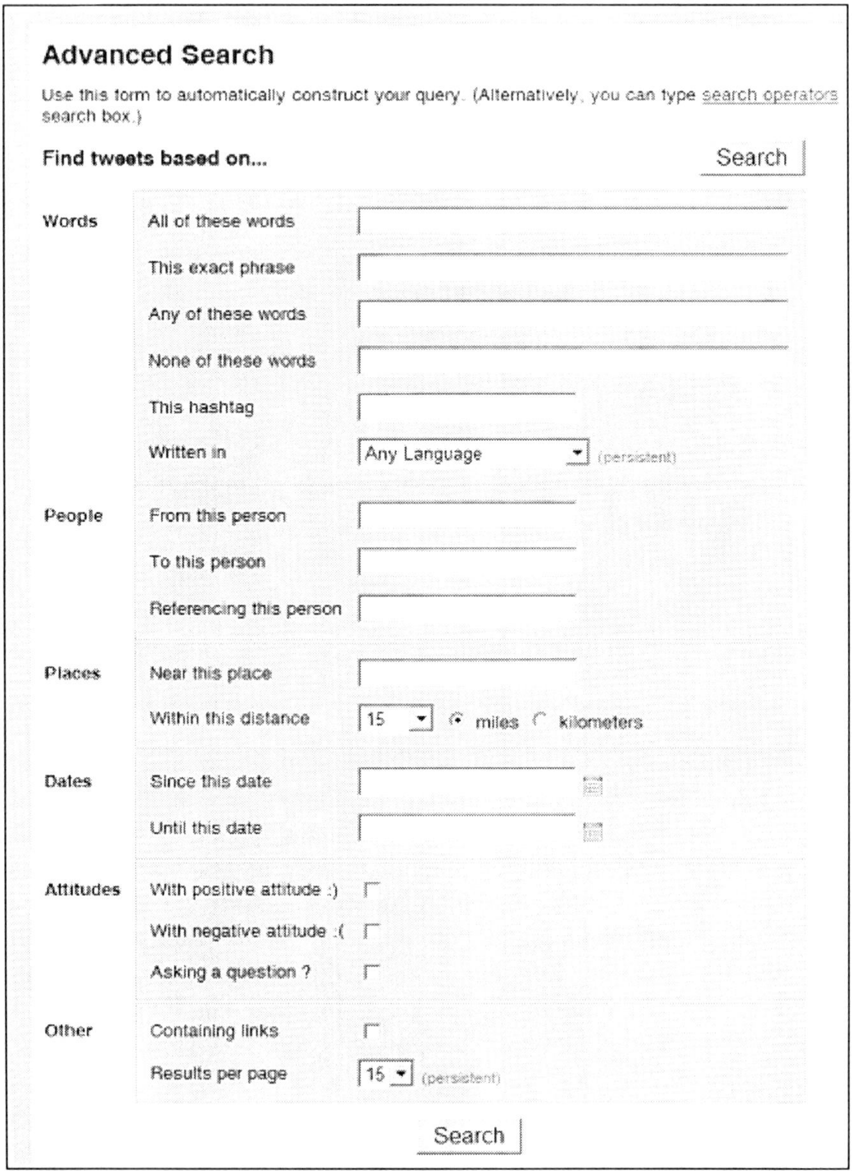

Expand your search with third-party applications

An array of free, useful services can help you navigate Twitter. Here's the cream of the crop:

1) TwitterCounter (http://twittercounter.com)

TwitterCounter computes a Twitter user's worldwide rank based on how many followers they have. It lists the top 1,000 Twitterers, but each individual user can always look up their own rank. It's a great place to search out people you'll want to follow on Twitter.

2) Twellow (http://twellow.com)

Twellow is sort of the Yellow Pages for Twitter. Basically, it categorizes Twitter users by their professions. If you're interested in networking with journalists, as an example, just double-click on that category and a list of people is displayed. The only thing to keep in mind is that Twellow only shows those who have registered with the service, so the results do not include every person in Twitter.

That being said, the application is growing in popularity, and thousands of folks are already using Twellow. More than 7,000 Twitter users are categorized in sports, along with more than 35,000 authors and writers.

3) Twibs (http://twibs.com)

Twibs offers an impressive directory of businesses on Twitter. It features a special section showcasing prominent businesses, and you can search for a specific company alphabetically.

If these four don't serve your needs, plenty of other Twitter directories and ranking applications are available. Just do a search on "Twitter Directories."

One more application important to mention here is Twollow (http://twollow.com). Twollow is hot because it enables you to:

- Automatically follow people based on your keywords.
- Quickly build a follower base.
- Discover other Twitterers with similar interests.
- Track what people are saying about your business.

Twollow even has a nifty free demo on its Web site. A free trial is available, then it costs $5.99 a month to use five keywords.

4) TwitterHolic (http://twitterholic.com)

TwitterHolic is similar to TwitterCounter, but does not provide as much functionality. However, the follower counts are fairly accurate, and you can search for yourself or any other Twitter user to see how they measure up.

User-generated directories

In addition to third-party applications, there are also niche directories. Here are a few:

- **A Directory of Book Trade People by Jennifer Tribe** (http://highspotinc.com/blog/2008/12/a-directory-of-book-trade-people-on-twitter)

This directory includes publishers, authors, literary agents, libraries, and virtually everyone else involved with books. If you're in the book trade business, all you have to do to be added to the list is send Jennifer a message—@jennifertribe, not a direct message.

- **Find and Follow Top Business Execs on Twitter** (http://exectweets.com)

ExecTweets has a massive directory of business executives who are using Twitter. You can search all executives or by industry (Government & Education, Health Care, Media/Advertising/PR, Retail, Technology, etc). It also has a featured and a most popular listing. You can even request that an executive be added.

- **WeFollow: Twitter Directory and Search (http://wefollow.com)**

WeFollow is a directory of Twitter users organized by interests. Find Twitter celebrities, actors, TV personalities, or new Twitter friends in your area.

More niche directories are showing up every day. Just search under "Twitter Niche Directories," or try searching for a specific niche.

Now you have people to follow, next you'll start building your followers.

Tweak your background

There's nothing wrong with using one of Twitter's standard backgrounds to get started. But by customizing your background, you can create a unique Twitter identity. And if you're using the site as a business tool, a customized background will help you get a lot more mileage from Twitter.

- **Personal and professional branding:** A customized background helps you develop and enhance your brand. Your Twitter background is prime real estate—don't let it go to waste.
- **Additional contact information:** If you have a blog, a Web site, a Facebook page, and so forth, you can add those links to a customized background. (The link won't be clickable; you'll only be able to show the link text.)
- **Forge an identity:** By creating a personalized background, you're helping potential followers get to know you. Whoever you are, whatever you do, you can use your creativity to spotlight yourself.
- **Compel potential followers:** Your profile is the first stop your potential followers will make before clicking on the "follow" button. Don't give them a reason to pass you by.

If you're still wondering why this is so important, take a look at some of the creative, unique, and inspiring backgrounds Twitterers are using:

Doug Cone (@nullvariable)
http://twitter.com/nullvariable

A Web designer and consultant, Doug Cone's Twitter profile is fun, cool, informative, and wildly creative.

Justine Ezeraik (@ijustine)
http://twitter.com/ijustine

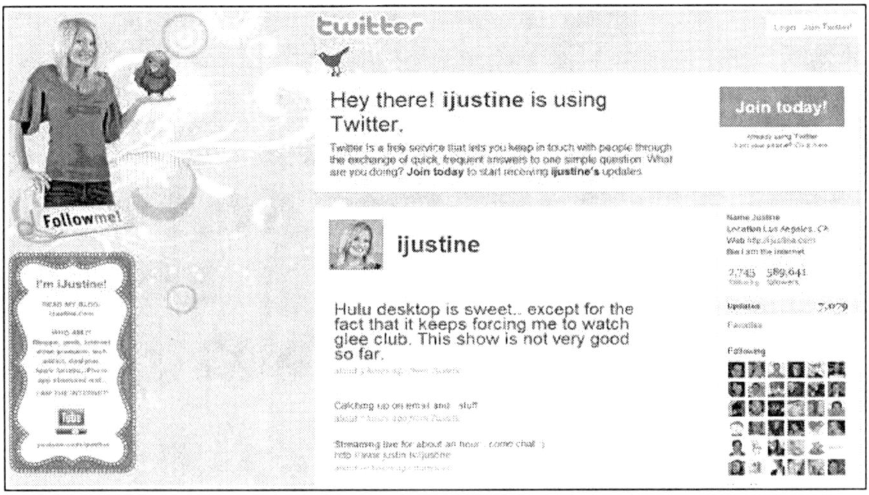

Internet video producer and media star Justine Ezeraik's Twitter background is witty, visually appealing, personable, and fun. With more than 589,000 followers, Justine definitely has an audience.

Jason Keath (@jakrose)
http://twitter.com/jakrose

Social media director, consultant, and speaker Jason Keath's Twitter background is bright, attention-grabbing, and visually interesting.

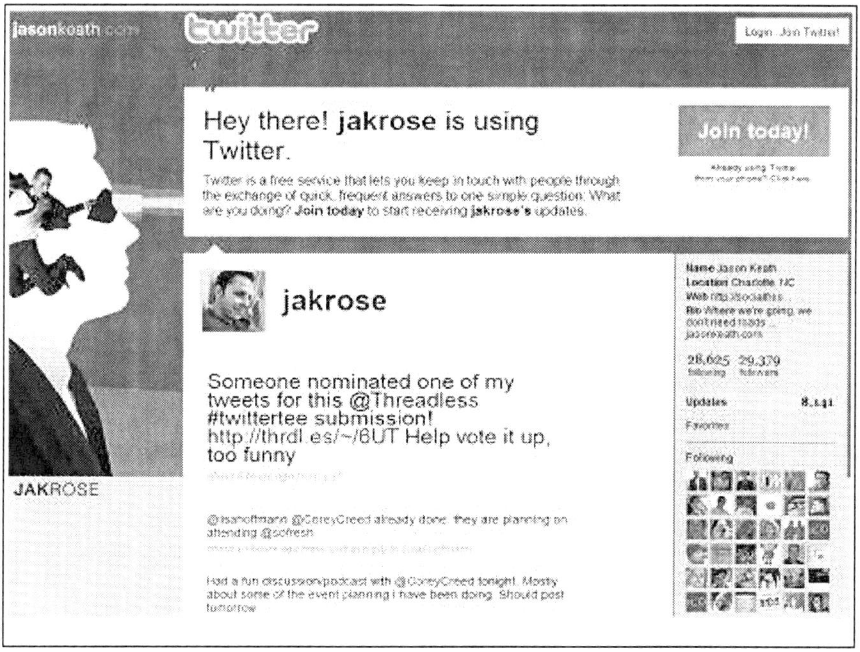

What elements do these three examples have in common? They're all:

- Unique
- Attractive
- Creative
- Informative
- Personal

When you compare these backgrounds with the generic few that Twitter offers, you should be able to see what customizing a background for your profile can do for you. Besides, it's a heck of a lot more fun. But how do you customize your background?

You needn't be an artist or pay someone a hefty fee for a professional-looking Twitter background. Several companies and individuals design custom Twitter backgrounds for as little as $25.

If you're interested in doing it yourself, customizable templates are available. Before deciding which method you'll use to develop a customized background, consider the goals you want your profile to achieve.

Consider what a profile can do

Before moving ahead with creating your background, you should spend a few minutes considering exactly what you want to get out of it. That way, whether you choose a template, create your background yourself, or hire a professional, you'll have a far better idea of what you need. That will give you a clearer path to developing a background that will work for you.

So, what should your profile do for you?

- **Develop and enhance your brand:** If you already have an online presence, you'll want to strike a balance between your Twitter background and your other online identities. Keeping your colors, design, and logo consistent with your Web site or blog is a good idea.
- **Personalize your background:** We've already talked about what type of picture you should use on your profile, but now consider whether the picture you're using will match the overall design and tone of your background. If, for example, the picture you've chosen is a serious studio shot, but your background is flamboyant and fun, you'll probably want to change photos. Choose a style and see it through—from the design to your photo to your bio.
- **Give contact information:** Twitter is meant to be a conversation tool, and yes, most of that conversation happens within Twitter. But that doesn't mean it's the only place you

can connect with your readers. Do you have a blog? A Web site? Let them know the URLs. Basically, let your readers know where they can find you on the Internet outside of Twitter.

- **Show your style:** While having an attractive profile might not guarantee that you'll gain additional followers, an unattractive one will surely limit your chances of growing the following you want. With this in mind, your background and overall profile should be visually pleasing. Be creative and have fun.
- **Speak to your audience:** Above all, your profile should speak to your intended audience. This encompasses your design, your colors, your picture, the tone of your writing, and even the information you include. Who is your intended audience?
  - **Family and friends:** This audience is the easiest. These are the people who know you best, so you can really have fun. Your profile should truly be a reflection of you, your likes, and the way you live your life.
  - **Current and potential clients or customers:** You know your business and products better than anyone else. What information will your clients and customers be looking for? What type of information will interest them? What will engage them so they stick around? If you're unsure, check out other Twitter pages from similar businesses and see what is and isn't working.
  - **Fans:** If you're in the public sector, such as a musician, author, or actor, you need to think about what your fans will want to know about you and what you do. Then combine that with what you're comfortable with. A musician might show pictures from recent performances, while an author could display recent book covers.
- Knowing who your prospective audience is and what they care about is a great starting point. If you're in doubt, just check out other Twitter pages—you're sure to get plenty of ideas for inspiration in creating your own image.

Now that you have an idea of what your overall profile should accomplish, you can begin to plan what it should look like. Then you can decide how you want to develop your background.

Do-it-yourself backgrounds

Making your own Twitter background isn't rocket science. For people who like to show off their creativity, it's a no-brainer.

Load up Twitter on your computer and select a random person's page. See the center of the screen? The white posting area? That section belongs to Twitter, and you can't change it. Therefore, you'll be focusing on the space around the center.

Tips for creating your design

Designing or choosing an image to use on your background can be fun, but there are a few points to remember:

- Go for larger images if possible. If the image is too small it will tile (be repeated) across the page, and the result is usually ugly.
- Remember that Twitter's logo occupies a small portion of the screen, and the user navigation menu consumes more space. If your image is complicated near the top, the background may look overly busy.
- Above all, remember where your information is going to go. The left-hand column and the header is where you'll be able to insert information. The center section belongs to Twitter.

Create a basic full-page background

Here's how to create a basic full-page background. The following instructions work in most cases, although the results might appear different on different computers with varying screen resolutions:

- **Select your image-editing software.** If you have a PC, it probably has image-editing software included. Microsoft Paint, which comes bundled with Windows, works just fine.
- **Be creative.** Select or create the image you want for your background. Make sure the image isn't so small that it tiles

across the screen. Your image should be around 1,600 pixels wide by 1,200 pixels tall. This is large enough to prevent tiling in nearly all resolutions.
- If you'd like to build a left-hand column for contact information, additional links, and so forth, ensure it's not too large. If the left column is too wide, it will be partially obscured. A width of 235 pixels usually works fine.
- When you're satisfied with the design, save the file as a JPG, GIF, or PNG file, ensuring it's smaller than 800 kilobytes.

Now, upload your new background to your Twitter account:

- Sign in to Twitter.
- Click on "Settings" in the upper-right corner.
- Click on the "Design" tab.
- At the bottom of this screen, click on the button "Change Background Image."
- At the top of this screen, you'll see a text field. Next to the text field is a "Browse" button. Click on that.
- Locate your saved file and double-click it.
- Leave the "Tile Background" checkbox empty. Otherwise your image will repeat across the screen.
- Click "Save Changes."
- Click on the "Profile" link at the top of page to check out how it looks. If you're satisfied, you're finished.
- If the spacing is off, or you don't like how something looks, then alter the original file to your specifications and upload again. It might take several tries before things look exactly right.

This no-fuss, no-muss method will give you a customized background with the content, colors, and anything else you want to have there. But depending on your skill and the amount of time you have available, you might prefer to go another route. You can get the look of a custom-created background by using one of the many third-party Twitter template backgrounds available. Even better, most of them are free.

Twitter templates

The explosion of Twitter users has spawned countless third-party Twitter services providing background templates. There are many styles available, most of which you can further customize. Here are six popular sites where you can find free Twitter background templates:

- **My Tweet Space** (http://mytweetspace.com)

My Tweet Space offers a simple approach to developing personalized backgrounds. Users can add graphics, play with text, and create left-hand text columns. And, if you log in with Twitter, My Tweet Space will automatically update your background. It's minimal effort with a huge payoff.

- **TwitBacks** (http://twitbacks.com)

TwitBacks is a popular Web site that specializes in left-hand column backgrounds. It offers plenty of free templates, and it's easy to make alterations so you can create exactly the look you want.

- **TweetStyle** (http://tweetstyle.com)

TweetStyle has it all: free templates, paid service, and plenty of blog articles chock-full of information about creating backgrounds.

- **TwitterBacks** (http://twitterbacks.com)

TwitterBacks has a set of templates that can help even the least creative person develop the perfect background. Its templates are in PhotoShop form.

- **TwitterGallery** (http://twittergallery.com)

If you're looking for super easy with lots of choices, then you'll want to check out TwitterGallery. It has a directory of themes, from colors to categories, in which to find the ideal background template. Installing is even simpler. Click the "install" button, log into Twitter, and the background is placed for you.

- **Free Twitter Designer** (http://freetwitterdesigner.com)

You can create a professional theme easily with Free Twitter Design's image editor.

As great as these templates are, there are times when nothing else will do but a completely customized background. If this is the case for you, and you don't mind paying a fee, skilled designers can create exactly what you want.

Professionally created Twitter backgrounds

Hiring a professional designer to create your Twitter background certainly has its benefits. They'll tailor your design to your needs, incorporate your brand into the design (such as your logo or slogan), and they know the Twitter ropes and can fix any possible malfunctions that might pop up. Plus, some of these designers are truly innovative.

Here are five professionals creating quite a following with their artistic Twitter background designs:

- **Trifecta Backgrounds** (http://trifectabackgrounds.com)

Trifecta Backgrounds' slogan is "Increase your followers and prove your credibility so people will listen. ... Who else wants a kick-ass Twitter background to quickly propel you to the Twitter Elite?"

With a splashy Web site, a client testimonial video, and a few links to Twitter backgrounds they've completed, it's apparent the folks at Trifecta Backgrounds know what they're doing. They deliver within a week. While their price of $127 is higher than the other four listed, they're still within a reasonable range for the service they offer.

- **Twitter Image.com** (http://twitterimage.com)

Twitter Image.com states it will create a background that makes you stand out from the crowd. The fee at the time of this writing was $100. The site also offers quite a few free Twitter background templates that anyone can download. You can view pages and pages of examples.

- **Custom Twitter Background** (http://customtwitterbackground.com)

Custom Twitter Background is priced in the mid range of the companies shown here. The company offers fully customized backgrounds for $67. The company promises to create a background that makes a statement and stands out. Like the other companies, Custom Twitter Background has a gallery of its work available, as well as several testimonials.

- **My Tweet Space** (http://mytweetspace.com)

My Tweet Space, the same Web site that offers free templates, also has a fully customizable background service to help you creatively and efficiently express your brand and image on Twitter. For $59, the company will design a background that shows "who you really are."

- **Logos for Web sites** (http://logosforwebsites.com)

This company is the least expensive of the five, charging a nominal $25 fee for a custom background. It also designs logos for about $30. While the Web site doesn't have very many examples of its Twitter work, it does have plenty of examples of logos they've created.

Whether you decide to create your own background, use a template, or hire a design professional to build one for you, knowing what you want to achieve will make the entire process easier. A custom background tells the Twitter world to pay attention to you, so it's worth the effort.

Here's the background I created for my Twitter account, WeberBooks, which features my book covers on the left panel:

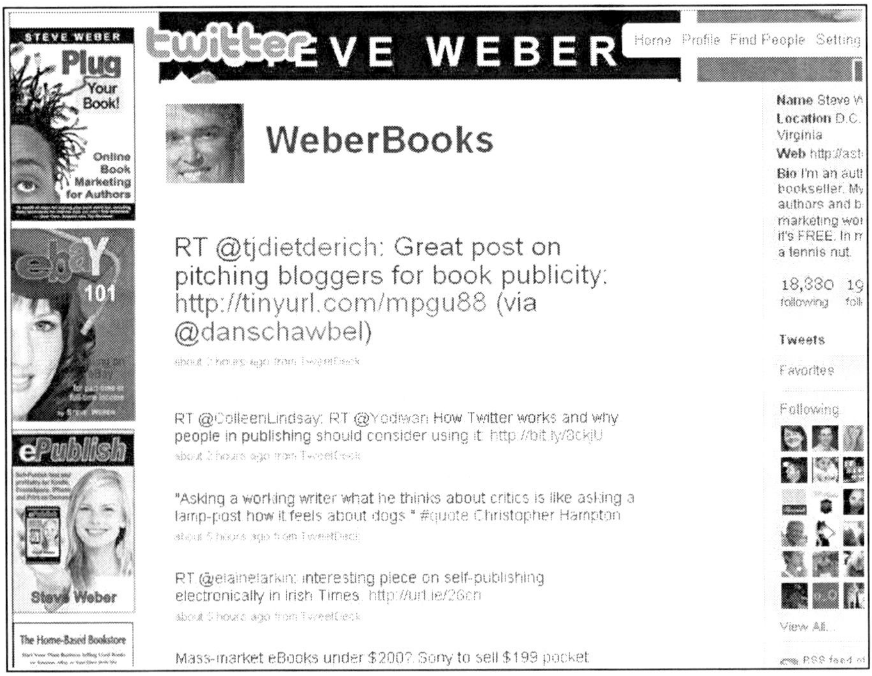

Build your following

Now that you've plunged into Twitter, it's time to build on your success. For business tweeters, the rationale for building a following is simple: Strength in numbers. You don't know exactly who is going to be of help to you, or even who is willing to help. The larger your pool of followers, the greater chance you'll achieve the results you want.

Follow these 14 steps to gaining a massive following:

1. Follow highly followed Twitterers

Search out opinion leaders with large numbers of followers. Not just anyone, but those who fall within your sphere of interest. The benefits to following someone who already has a massive following are many:

- Many use an auto-follow feature. You can be assured of being accepted into the fold. When you follow them, they'll follow you.
- Once you're following a heavyweight, watch and learn. See how they use Twitter—how often they tweet, and the kinds of tweets they use. Watching successful tweeters will provide lots of inspiration on creating your own success.
- When potential followers look at your profile, they'll see you're following some folks with crazy high rankings. Success breeds success.

2. Tweet the high-rankers

Send these folks a tweet. Even if they miss the message or don't reply, dropping their name can help your credibility. It can tempt a few folks to check your profile and follow you. While you're tweeting, say something worthwhile; you don't want to look like a spammer.

3. Join conversations

Each day you should be searching for and jumping into the conversations that interest you. Look at the right-hand sidebar on the Twitter home page. There, you'll see a listing of that day's popular conversations. Scan the tweets from the high-ranking Twitterers you follow. Join in the conversations, and you'll gain wider exposure.

4. Tweet consistently

Even if your long-range plan isn't to tweet every day, you should tweet several days per week, especially while you're growing your follower bank. You want your tweets to be interesting, funny, and engaging so people will keep coming back.

5. Tweet what you know

What this really means is that you want to establish yourself as an expert in your industry or area of interest. Your tweets will be found by people who share your interest—just the folks you want as followers. You can establish yourself as an expert in a couple of ways:

- Create original tweets based on the subject in which you're trying to establish yourself.
- Search for the best tweets on that subject. Then reply to those tweets, or retweet them. This can get you noticed and build your following.

6. Use pictures and other media

Tweet a great one-liner with a link to a picture related to the one-liner. These can be humorous, serious, opinionated, whatever. The point is to engage your audience and get them to not only click on the link to view the picture or video, but to then respond with their thoughts.

7. Link, link, and link

Link to more than just pictures and video. If you read an interesting article, tweet a link to it. You can do this with anything you can find on the Internet, so keep your eyes open for things that grab your interest, are relevant, and are worthwhile.

8. Advertise your Twitter identity

Expand your reach by advertising your Twitter account on your Web site, blog, and other social networking sites. Give all of your audience the ability to easily find and follow you on Twitter.

9. Submit to Twitter directories

Take the time to submit your Twitter account to various Twitter directories and services. You'll not only get a link to your Twitter account, but you'll then be in places other Twitterers use to find folks to follow. Here are a few directories to get you started:

- Wefollow (http://wefollow.com)
- TwitterHolic (http://twitterholic.com)
- Twibs (http://twibs.com)
- Twellow (http://twellow.com)
- Just Tweet It (http://justtweetit.com)

10. Ask for help

Ask people on Twitter to help you get noticed. They can retweet some of your tweets, for example. If you're posting a particularly awesome tweet today, add "Please retweet!" to the end. (Don't do this too often, or it will get tiresome.)

Add a Twitter button or widget to your Web site, blog, Facebook or MySpace page. See http://twitter.com/goodies/widgets.

Search for popular blogs in your niche, and write a guest post, including your Twitter name.

12. Ask people to follow

On your blog, your Web site, and other social networking sites, just say “Hey, I’m on Twitter. Follow me!” It works, and there’s nothing to lose by asking.

13. Follow your followers

As soon as you begin getting followers, follow everyone who follows you. You can change your mind later, but when you’re beginning to find your audience it can really help you develop a foothold. Your exposure will widen, and that’s one of the key factors to growing your audience.

14. Unfollow stale tweeters

As the number of your followers grows, you’re going to reach a point where you’ll have to make some decisions. You’ll have some tweeters that fall in the high-ranking group, and you should probably keep following them.

Keep in mind that Twitter places some limitations on accounts, to keep spammers at bay. Generally, you’re free to follow up to 2,000 people. To go over 2,000, you must have an equal number of people following you. Twitter also imposes daily limits on the number of new people you can follow—it’s usually about 500.

Tweet effectively

Have you ever sat in a room, with lots of people around you, chattering about different topics? That's exactly what Twitter is like, a cocktail party. All those different conversations can make it hard to focus. At a real-life cocktail party, you can huddle in a corner with one or two people for a minute, then scoot across the room. On Twitter, you can do much the same. Learning the ropes of effective tweeting will enhance the conversations you join in on, and at the same time, give you the knowledge you need to block the distractions you're not interested in.

What to know about tweeting

Twitter can be a fabulous tool, but successfully using this tool is another story. While the learning curve for Twitter isn't steep, it can seem daunting. To get the knack of effective tweeting, you've got to consider:

- Conversing vs. broadcasting.
- How to effectively communicate.
- Twitter-specific jargon and techniques.
- Twitter etiquette.

Broadcasting vs. conversing

Have you thought about the differences between "broadcasting" and "conversing"? You can't broadcast with a telephone, and you can't converse with a megaphone. Knowing the difference is key to your success on Twitter.

Remember that room filled with chatting people? If you stood in the middle of that room and shouted a message that everyone else could hear, that's broadcasting. By contrast, conversing directs your message toward one conversation, and only those folks involved.

Broadcasting

When you're logged into Twitter, you see the question "What are you doing?" above a text box. If you type in your tweet with no preceding characters, and then click "update," you're broadcasting. If you have no followers, you can be assured that nobody is listening—unless someone stumbles across your words in a search.

If you've attracted followers, your broadcasted tweet will go to all of them. Broadcasting is a great way to put a message out there. But you can't broadcast all the time, if you want people to pay attention. Here are some guidelines for when to broadcast:

- **When you have something worthwhile to broadcast.** This could include things like a contest you're holding, an announcement, or alerting followers to information in your niche.
- **When you focus on the specific topic that speaks to your brand.** If you're establishing yourself as an expert in a subject, then many of your followers will be following you because of your knowledge.
- **When you want to drive traffic elsewhere.** Maybe you want people to visit your blog, Facebook page or Web site, or perhaps to a video you've posted to YouTube. Go ahead, shout about it. But make it good.

Conversing

Holding a conversation in Twitter is just as easy as broadcasting, but there's one difference you can see: "@". Remember that text box on your Twitter home page? The one that asks you what you are doing? Instead of typing in your tweet straight, you'll precede it with: "@username."

This focuses your tweet toward that specific person. You're either entering into a conversation that person has started or is involved in, or you're starting a new conversation. Other people can read it, but they know you're talking to @username.

The distinction between broadcasting and conversing is important, even if you're on Twitter mainly for business. In most cases, you want to balance your broadcasts with conversations, so you're viewed as someone both with interesting information to share, and as someone involved and interested in the Twitter community. That's not to say you can't be successful by primarily broadcasting messages. If the type of information you're broadcasting is informative, interesting, and engaging, then you'll do much better than a spammer who repeats the same promotional material time after time.

Before you broadcast a message, ask yourself: "Will this tweet give something of value to my followers, or am I only pimping myself, my company, or my product?" If your followers can glean value from your message, then go ahead and broadcast it. But remember, if you get repetitive and tiresome, your followers will lose interest and leave.

Tweet with impact

Communicating on Twitter is a skill you must develop and polish. Here are some tips on tweeting with maximum impact:

- **Don't be vague.** Every tweet you write should have a focus. Use that limit of 140 characters to sharpen your mind and message. Being too vague creates confusion, especially within a series of replies. When replying to another tweet, in addition to using the "@" symbol, include a reminder of the tweet you're responding to.
- **Keywords are good.** Pack your tweets with keywords, and you needn't worry about being vague. Your followers will get your point, and new followers will easily find you. Win, win.
- **Be interesting.** Sounds obvious, but requires effort. Even mundane tweets can be spiced up with a little thought. And you needn't be clever, humorous, witty, and unique—you just need to *look* that way.

- **Share information.** Instead of just answering the "What are you doing?" question, think of more questions:

  What are you thinking?

  What do you want to do?

  What is the funniest/scariest/coolest thing you've seen/read/heard lately?

  What has you excited (or any other emotion) right now?

  What are you most looking forward to?

  What was the best thing about your day?

  What's your biggest pain in the butt?

  Mix it up. Have fun.

- **Be interactive.** Take the time to interact with other tweeters, even just a few times a week. Remember, it's not all about you, you, you. What people really care about is them. So make it about them sometimes.

When you deliver great content combined while interacting with the Twitter community, you'll find your Twittering gets plenty of results.

Understanding Twitter's secret codes

Every club has its own lingo. Here's a quick guide to what you need to know for Twitter:

- **Reply (@):** To direct a conversation toward a specific user, or to continue an existing conversation with a specific user, you start your tweet with "@username." The Web-based interface, as well as nearly every Twitter application, has a reply icon you can click to automatically add the prefix. Without the prefix, you're broadcasting, which doesn't work all that well if you're trying to continue a conversation with a specific Twitterer.

- **Direct Message (DM).** The letters "DM" refer to a "direct message." Basically, a DM is a private message that only the sender and recipient can see. To send a direct message to another user, you'll use the prefix "d" followed by the receiver's username. If a subject isn't meant for public consumption, or if you and the other person have sent several replies back and forth, moving to direct messages make sense.
- **Retweet (RT):** A retweet is simply repeating a tweet already sent. You can retweet anyone you like, or even yourself (sparingly, please). When retweeting, it's good form to leave the original tweeter's username and exact words intact. The great thing about retweeting is it allows you and others to share knowledge, and creates more exposure for both the original tweeter and the person retweeting. You can retweet a message simply by copying and pasting it, adding "RT @username." Many Twitter tools have a "retweet" button, making it quicker and easier.
- **Hashtag (#):** Hashtags allow any user to create a categorization of tweets that then can be found through a search function. To create a hashtag, use the prefix "#" before the keyword term for which you want to create a category. Then folks can contribute their own tweets to the same hashtag. Later, people can use the "#keyword" in search functions to find all tweets associated with it. To learn more about hashtags: http://twitter.pbworks.com/Hashtags.
- **Tiny URL (http://tiny.cc):** When including links in your tweets, you might find yourself becoming frustrated with Twitter's 140-character limit. After all, some URLs are ridiculously long, and could easily take up most of your message. The solution: Shorten your URLs. Simply copy the link you want to shorten, go to Tiny URL, and paste the link into the text box. Then click "Tiny it!" and you'll receive a new, shortened URL that will take up far less space in your tweet. There are plenty of URL shorteners out there, and most of the third-party Twitter tools have one-click URL shortening.

- **TwitterSnooze** (http://twittersnooze.com): What if you're following a few people who are, for whatever reason, driving you crazy with their too-frequent tweets? You can unfollow them, but some people take it as an insult. The solution: Hit the snooze button. TwitterSnooze allows you to take a break from anyone for up to 30 days. Visit TwitterSnooze, type in your information, and enjoy the relief.

Twitter etiquette. Really?

Although Emily Post hasn't published a Twitter guide, there are several unwritten rules. Stuff that's good to know:

1. **Twitter is a conversation.** Ask questions, contribute interesting information, and have fun.
2. **Don't be creepy.** Don't be too familiar with folks you don't know.
3. **It's quality, not quantity.** A few good tweets go a long way.
4. **Use good grammar when you can.** Sure, lots of folks substitute **4** for **for** and **2** for **to**. But people can only stomach so many shortcuts. If you can't say it in 140 characters, rethink your tweet.
5. **Be discreet.** If you wouldn't say something to someone's face, don't say it on Twitter.
6. **When someone follows you, follow them.** If later you find they're not supplying valuable information, you can unfollow them.
7. **Don't be slanderous, rude, or cruel.** It's unattractive, and you could get yourself in trouble, too.
8. **Tweet smart.** If you called in sick this morning, don't tweet about your shopping trip the same morning. It's not worth getting fired.

Use common sense and show some respect while you're tweeting, and you'll be OK.

Get down to business

Now we're getting down to brass tacks. Here we'll discuss tips for engaging your audience, enhancing and promoting your brand, connecting with your customers, and using Twitter for research.

Using Twitter to engage your audience

Everything you do in Twitter requires connecting with other people. If you can't engage them, it won't matter how many broadcasts you send out or how brilliant your Web site is. People just won't care.

Here are four ways to engage your audience:

1. **Ask for introductions.** When you have a decent number of followers, send weekly or monthly broadcasts asking people to introduce themselves. Then, respond. Perhaps you can't personally respond to 100 folks, but tweet back to a few who made you laugh or think. Then tweet a thank-you note for everyone who participated.
2. **Poll your followers.** Pick one day a week to poll your followers on a topic in your field. "What do you all think of XXX? My opinion is XXX." That gets a conversation going and builds your audience.
3. **Get feedback from your followers.** And be prepared for constructive criticism. Ask your followers their opinion on any subject relating to your business or your product.
4. **Have followers ask the question.** Send a broadcast once a week or so saying, "Have a question about XXX?

Fire away!" Or, "I'm ready to answer questions about XXX."

The more someone sees your name, your business name, and the name of your product, the more recognition you get. Much of what you decide to do will be oriented to your brand's niche. However, there are basic universal techniques.

Twitter for brand enhancement and promotion

1. **Study your competitors.** Search Twitter to find your competitors, and take a long look at what they're doing to promote their products or services. View their past tweets, and click their links to discover what's working for them. Take notes on the methods you like, especially those that mesh with your marketing plan.
2. **Offer free content.** Offering valuable content builds loyalty with your followers. Your audience will begin to trust you, and they'll bring their friends to you. The type of free content you choose to offer will greatly depend on your niche. Web site designers might offer a few free templates for creating a home page, while authors might give away a story or an e-book. Be creative.
3. **Become known as an expert.** Let the Twitter universe know you are an expert in your niche. Send out relevant tweets with relevant links, answer questions, write longer posts on your blog and link to it in your tweets.
4. **Keep your followers informed.** Are you going to be at an event that other people might like to visit? Signing books over the weekend? Has your company or product just received an awesome review? Let your followers know about it.
5. **Provide exemplary customer service.** If your clients, customers, and fans have questions, answer them. Troubleshoot complaints. Show them you believe in your business by being present. Whether you're a sole proprietor or part of a large company, find ways to offer top support to the people who purchase your products. This might mean directing customers to another source to get their

issue taken care, or it might mean that you handle it personally.

6. **Promote to increase your brand and sales.** There are many, many ways you can use Twitter to further your marketing plan. Here are a few thoughts to get you started:

Offer Twitter-exclusive deals and discounts

You can offer to give any of your followers some type of discount on your service or product. People love deals, sales, and discounts. To tweet a deal, just broadcast details to your followers. Some companies even have a separate Twitter account, just to tweet special deals:

Amazon.com: http://twitter.com/amazondeals

Dell Computer: http://twitter.com/delloutlet

GoDaddy.com: http://twitter.com/GoDaddyDeals

Also check out CheapTweet, at http://cheaptweet.com, which compiles special-deal tweets and ranks them by user ratings and Twitter conversations.

More ideas:

- **Use links to offer deals and discounts.** Instead of the deal being on Twitter, you're using a tweet to link to it. You can create a free download on your Web site, or post a sale coupon, and then send out a tweet with a link to drive traffic to your site.
- **Build buzz.** Be the first to reveal relevant information about your field. Once folks realize they'll hear it first from you via Twitter, they'll pay attention.
- **Offer contests and giveaways.** Hold contests on a consistent basis to engage your audience and promote your product. If you're an author, for example, you could give away copies of books, bookmarks, and other promotional materials.

- **Conduct Twitter presentations.** Either once a week or once a month, invite all your followers to a Twitter gabfest. The presentation can be about a specific topic relating to your niche, one of your products, an author talk, a Q&A, or whatever you think will generate interest. You can promote the upcoming conversation on your blog and Web site, and announce it a few days ahead of time on Twitter. The day of the event, be prepared to check in with Twitter a lot so you can answer questions and immerse yourself in the ongoing conversation.
- **Keep tabs on what works.** Monitor everything you do and keep your eye on what techniques show results. Which tweets brought the most responses? The most followers? Most retweets? This will help you target which areas, topics, and promotion efforts are most worthwhile for you to continue. And this information will help you streamline all of your efforts and gain the best results with less energy.
- **Don't stop.** Many people make the mistake of hitting the brakes when find success. This is the last thing you want to do. Folks have short memories, and they'll easily gravitate toward someone else who fights harder for their attention. Don't rest. Keep promoting your company, your products, and your brand by focusing on what's working, and keep looking for new avenues.

Connecting with customers via Twitter

There's a good chance many of your customers, clients, and fans are already using Twitter. This gives you a perfect opportunity to reconnect with them and show how awesome you and your business are. How do you find them and connect?

Use the Twitter search function to scan for customers. Search under your name, your company's name, and your product names. Then, spend some time reading through the results and seeing what folks have to say. Starting here, you can:

- Introduce yourself.
- Enter conversations.

- Help solve problems.
- Let them know you're on Twitter and will be tweeting about your business and your products.

Once customers begin following you, you can do even more to increase their satisfaction and promote your brand:

1. **Provide updates about products.** As an example, one Twitter-savvy bakery tweets when it has fresh bread coming out of the oven.
2. **Offer promotions for your product.** Your current customers should be the first to know about anything special you have planned. This includes discounts, sneak peeks, contests, giveaways, and events.
3. **Listen and respond.** Find questions, possible issues, and opinions, letting your customers know you're interested in their experience and in keeping them as customers.
4. **Solicit feedback.** While bad feedback could be let loose in Twitter for the entire world to see, it's a risk worth taking. Asking your customers for feedback will give you information you can't get anywhere else. Even better, when you get great feedback, that information is also there for the world to see. Word-of-mouth advertising is the best you can get.

Connecting with your customers via Twitter is a win-win. Not only will it increase visibility for you and your business, but you'll be building valuable relationships and networking with the folks who are spending their money for your service. Take the time to get to know them, learn about their concerns, offer them valuable content, and they'll help you build your business—one tweet at a time.

Using Twitter as a research tool

Sure, Twitter is fun, but it's a real tool for building contacts and expanding your business. In short, it's a wickedly good research tool. Advice, opinions, concerns, rumors, news, and more is being passed around Twitter at lightning speed. You can use information from these tweets.

Let's think about what types of information are available, and how to find it.

Research current topics and trends

Twitter's search function, http://search.twitter.com, lets you discover what users are talking about now. These insights appear on Twitter first, not Google or CNN. For example, when US Airways Flight 1549 crashed into the Hudson River in January 2009, the first reports and pictures came from Twitter. When the Iranian government tried to block news coverage of election protests that summer, the world knew through Twitter. For weeks, the Twitter hashtag #Iranelection was the No. 1 topic.

Plug in an event, a topic, or a name, and wait for the results to pop up. Within minutes, you can have lots of up-to-the-minute data. To further refine your search, you can use hashtags in the advanced search menu. Just type in #(topic) and click "search."

Research your company and products

In addition to Twitter's regular search, you can automate your Twitter searches so you never miss who's saying what about you:

Monitter (http://monitter.com)

Monitter feeds three streams of up-to-the-second tweets to you as they happen. Type in a keyword or phrase at the top of each column, and then hit return. The live streams (as they literally are typed into Twitter) will pop up on the screen. This is an incredible way of keeping up on discussions about your business and your products. You can also download a widget to make it even simpler.

Tweetbeep (http://tweetbeep.com)

Tweetbeep is a lot like Google Alerts, except it's specifically for Twitter and therefore more timely. You can keep up with tweets that mention you, your products, your company, or anything at all. Signup is free and easy. Just type in your Twitter information along with your name and e-mail.

Research individuals

Using Twitter's search function, or any of the third-party directories, you can research individuals by locating all tweets that mention a specific name. Within Twitter's advanced search, you can put in additional information to refine your search.

To find out if an individual has identities on other social networking sites, you might want to check out FriendFeed, http://friendfeed.com. FriendFeed tracks an individual's activity across numerous social networking sites, such as LinkedIn, YouTube, and Facebook. You can view this data through FriendFeed, and therefore broaden your research.

You can set up an RSS feed for any of the searches you perform at Twitter.

Using Twitter to drive behavior

Driving behavior through Twitter starts with a tweet. Sure, that tweet might contain a link, but before anyone clicks on it, your message must be compelling. Further, when someone clicks on your link, you need valuable content at the destination if you want a reaction. The desired reaction might be a sale, or registration at your Web site. The question is, how do you get people to act?

- Offer a discount that ends within a certain period. If you want them to sign up for your mailing list, give them a reason to do so before they leave your site. For example, "The first 15 people who sign up will receive a $5 gas card."
- Contests are a good way to get people to join your list. Add a caveat to all of your contests that states, "By entering this contest, I'm giving permission to be added to So-and-So's mailing list."

The bottom line: Create a "I should do this now" feeling, both in your original tweet and in the linked site.

Tweeting at the next level

Now you've got the basics down. You know the ins and outs of Twitter, and now it's time to kick it up a notch. Here's how to start getting even more out of Twitter:

- **Consider outsourcing.** Twitter is fun and addictive, but it can consume lots of time. Should you have a ghostwriter—or in this case, a ghost-tweeter? Perhaps, but your helper should perform only certain Twitter functions, such as broadcasting and marketing. You've still got to be the one conversing with followers. Your followers will recognize if someone else is pretending to be you. Consider having two Twitter accounts —one used exclusively by you, and another account for your representative. Your followers would know which one is you.
- **Build a targeted opt-in e-mail list.** After you've built trust with your followers, send out direct messages inviting them to join your e-mail list. Clearly explain the benefits (downloadable reports, articles about your niche subject, discounts), and be sure to deliver those benefits. You'll expand your reach, and give your followers yet another way to get valuable and interesting information from you.
- **Tell everyone that you're on Twitter.** This means putting your Twitter address on your e-mail signature, your business cards, your Web site, your blog, and other social-networking sites where you have created an online identity.
- **Don't disappear on the weekends.** You don't have to be as active on Saturday and Sunday as you are the rest of the week, but pop in once or twice a couple of weekends per

month just to check in. As weird as it sounds, your followers want to believe that Twitter is fun for you. If you're visible only Monday through Friday, you don't look like you're having fun.

- **Use multiple Twitter accounts.** If you tweet about unrelated topics, or you want to keep a wall between your business tweets and social tweets, you may need another Twitter account—or two. That's fine, although Twitter requires a separate e-mail address for each account. Most third-party Twitter software makes it easy to switch between accounts, even on mobile devices.

Automate Twitter

You can save time on many of your Twitter tasks by using automation tools. These also can increase your effectiveness.

- **Automatically send a customized, direct message (DM) to a new follower.** Within the message you can have a short greeting, as well as a link to your Web site or blog, so your new followers have immediate content to digest. You're grabbing your new followers' attention fast, and increasing your exposure instantly. TweetLater.com's free basic service will let you send the same greeting to each of your new followers.
- **Automatically add blog posts to Twitter.** If you're a blogger, you'll see the appeal in having your blog posts appear on Twitter. Some options:

1. **Twitterfeed** (http://twitterfeed.com) makes this process very simple. All you have to do is register at the Web site, provide the URL for your blog's RSS feed, indicate when you want them to check your blog, and how often they should post your blog's feed to Twitter.
2. **Twitthis** (http://twitthis.com). Twitthis provides a Twitter button you can add to your blog or Web site. When Twitter users read your content, they can tweet about it with a click of a button, giving you more exposure.

- **Feed your tweets to your Facebook page.** This lets you update your Facebook page effortlessly. Once you have this set up, you can stop by Facebook just once a week or so. Get this feature directly through Facebook's application page: http://apps.facebook.com/twitter/
- **Use Twitter badges and widgets.** A Twitter badge is a button you add to your Web site, blog, Facebook, or MySpace account. It enables readers to easily tweet the title and link to your content. Twitter has complete instructions here: http://help.twitter.com/forums/10711/entries/15354.

Third-party Twitter applications

Here are the most popular and useful (and mostly free) third-party applications that can help you be more creative and effective on Twitter:

- **Twitpic** (http://twitpic.com). Allows you to easily share photos on Twitter, whether you're using your cellphone, your computer, or another third-party tool. You log into the free service using your Twitter credentials. Viewers of your photo may comment as a reply tweet.
- **Tweetdeck** (http://tweetdeck.com). A free program enabling users to send and receive tweets and view profiles. You can view a stream of tweets from any individual user and constantly search for names or other keywords. Available for a variety of computers and the iPhone.
- **Seesmic Desktop** (http://seesmic.com). Like Tweetdeck, Seesmic enables users to simultaneously view lists of followers or searches.
- **Twhirl** (http://twhirl.org). Twhirl is a Twitter client similar to Tweetdeck, and owned by the same company that provides Seesmic Desktop.

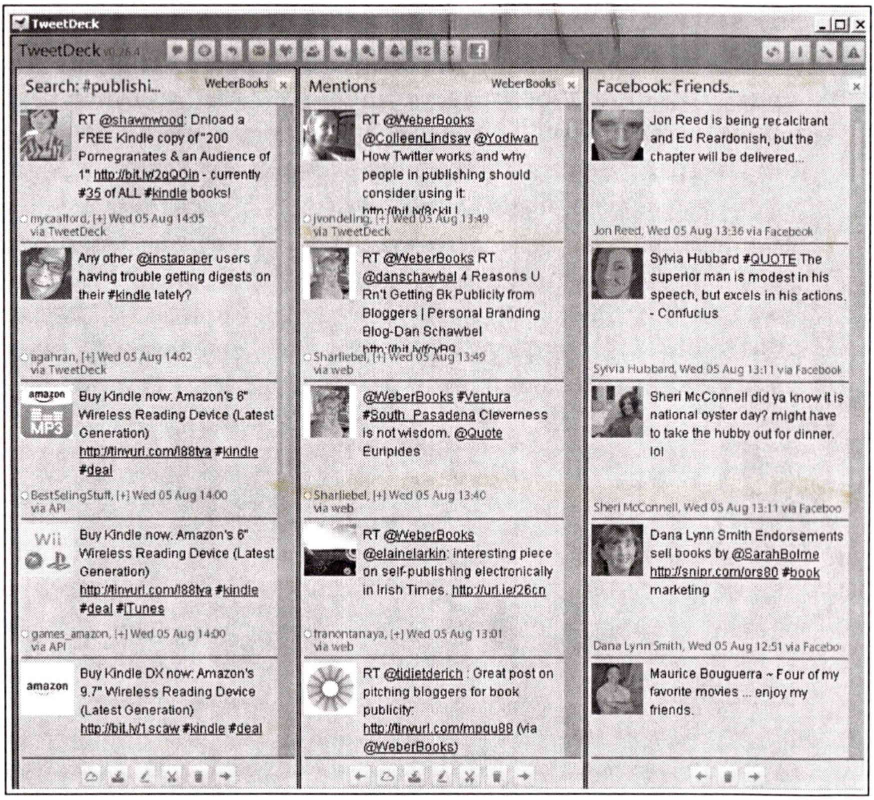

- **Twitturly** (http://twitturly.com). Twitturly's main function is to track in real time and rank the URLs people are talking about on Twitter. This is a free application.
- **Digsby** (http://digsby.com). Allows you to check e-mails and messages from Facebook, MySpace, and Twitter. You can also use Digsby to sign into instant-message accounts.
- **Twtpoll** (http://twtpoll.com). Twtpoll, with about 75,000 unique monthly visitors., is a feedback tool that helps you create and distribute polls on Twitter, Facebook, and other social-media sites. All you do is click on the "Create a Poll" button, type in the appropriate information on the following page, and click "Create a Poll" to get your poll out there. There's nothing to download because everything is run directly from the Twtpoll site. This is a free application.

- **Retweetist** (http://retweetist.com). With about 60,000 unique visitors per month, Retweetist shares whatever news is being retweeted extensively through Twitter. You can follow Retweetist (@Retweetist) to receive these updates via Twitter, or just check out the free site on a regular basis.
- **Tweepler** (http://tweepler.com). Tweepler has slightly more than 50,000 unique visitors each month and makes it easier to choose who to follow. It's a simple way to read the status of those you're considering following, and you can "ignore" those you don't wish to follow. With a simple, clean interface, Tweepler is free and easy to use.
- **Hellotxt** (http://hellotxt.com). Hellotxt has just over 45,000 unique visitors per month. Hellotxt posts your status updates from the Web, your mobile device, SMS, e-mail, or third-party applications through its API to more than 40 social networks. This allows you to update everyone, and everything, at once. Hellotxt is a free application.
- **TweetChat** (http://tweetchat.com). TweetChat is becoming more popular each week, so even though it didn't make the "most popular" count, its unique function is worth learning about. In a nutshell, TweetChat helps you ignore the rest of the Twitter world while you monitor and chat about one topic in "rooms" set up by TweetChat. It will also automatically add a hashtag for the room you are in, so the entire conversation will be searchable by that hashtag. This application is free. It can be useful for business-related chats like customer service.

Advanced business applications

Once you've realized the potential in Twitter, you'll want to check out some of the advanced applications that can maximize the benefits to your business. Some possibilities:

Twist (http://twist.flaptor.com)

Twist allows you to track trends on Twitter, just as Google Trends does for Google searches. Tweets are filtered into one-hour intervals, providing a visualization of what's popular among Twitter users. You can enter a phrase (topic) in the search box to see how frequent it appears over time, or several different topics separated by commas.

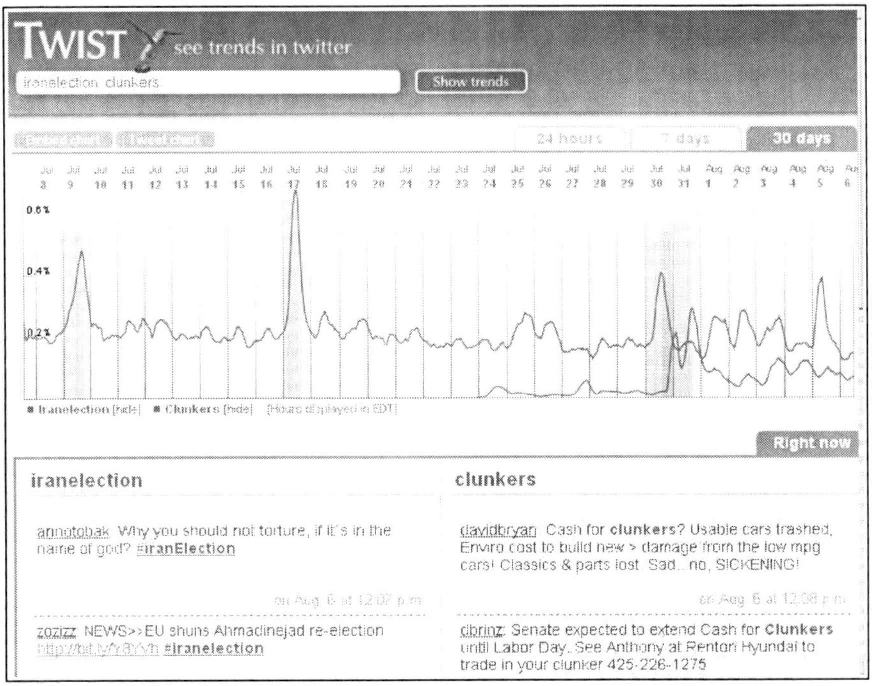

CoTweet (http://cotweet.com).

CoTweet is designed for corporate and government use. It allows multiple posters and multiple accounts. You can assign tweets to colleagues for follow-up. They'll be notified via e-mail, and the tweets will appear in their queue. After they've responded, you receive an e-mail containing their response along with the original tweet.

cotweet
Welcome, Kyle
Settings
Support
Results for
bubbo
34 minutes ago
OK. I'm in the CoTweet private beta! Getting set to integrate all our Twitter accounts. AdsNational + CoTweet = Win! http://cotweet.com ^MB
dalesmcd
about 1 hour ago
Eeennteresting! http://cotweet.com/ RT @espressojunky: Checking out CoTweet .. it's pretty damn cool!
jullonc
Testing cotweet, is cool! :D
ipad
@globovision Si quieren probar CoTweet avisenme con un reply y les envio 1 invitación que tengo... @Ford @Microsoft y @Twitterapi la usan
shopuptown
Just checking how cotweet works... could be a great time saver! Check out our new uptown
cotweet_support
@c3k I'll be able to look further into this tonight. Thanks for your patience. ^KS
c3k
@cotweet_support yup verified that I was using the correct settings + link and it still gives me the error...
cotweet_support
@RaccoonWillie Thanks! Very much appreciated. ^KS
HHRVB
@cotweet_support Thank you for the plug! I've received several inquiries since announcing your service at our recent SM Presentation. ^SE
seanpowell
@cotweet_support Got the latest invite and it worked! Thx!

Twitter unplugged

We've mastered the basics of Twitter, gaining a following, and tweeting at a high level. Now we'll explore using Twitter via a mobile device, such as a cellphone, BlackBerry or iPhone. There are both benefits and limitations to using a cellphone for Twitter, which is why most people use both their phone and a computer.

Tweeting with your phone

The founders of Twitter designed it to work with the cellphone "texting" service known as SMS. In fact, the 140-character limitation for tweets exists because that's the maximum length of a text message. But it doesn't really matter whether you or your followers use a desktop or Web-based application for Twitter. Tweets are delivered based on the recipient's account settings. And don't worry, registering your phone with Twitter won't give anyone access to your phone number. Even though your tweet may appear as a text on a follower's cellphone, your phone number isn't shown.

Mobility, of course, is the prime benefit of tweeting with your cellphone. You can tweet while you're out running errands, away on business trips, on vacation, or at a restaurant. Twitter can go just about anywhere. However, there are a few drawbacks to Tweeting on the go:

- If your cellphone carrier charges you for your text messaging, the same fees will apply to the tweets you send and receive. The fees can pile up quickly unless you have an unlimited text plan. (On the other hand, if your phone has

Web access, you can escape the fees by using Tweetdeck on the iPhone, for example. Yet another option is Twitter's mobile Web interface, http://m.twitter.com.)

- If you have a lot of followers, and you have all of their updates being sent to your phone, you'll have a very difficult time keeping up. However, you can use text commands to specify which users' updates you want sent to your phone. Section three of this chapter will explore phone text commands for Twitter.

Your decision on whether to use Twitter on your mobile device might depend on how often you're away from a computer, how flexible you want to be, and how comfortable you are with your cellphone in general.

Use Twitter with your cellphone

It's easy to set up your phone for Twitter. All you need is a computer with an Internet connection and a mobile device with either Web-based or text-messaging capabilities. Here's what you have to do:

1. Sign in to Twitter, and then click on the "Settings" link in the upper right-hand corner of the page.
2. The Settings page will pop up. Click on the "Devices" tab at the top of the new page. You'll see this page:
3. Enter your complete cellphone number, including your area code, in the "Mobile Phone" text box. If you live outside of the United States, precede your cell number with a "+" and your country's code.
4. Directly below the text box, you'll see this: *It's OK for Twitter to send txt messages to my phone. Standard rates apply.* Two things to notice here. As mentioned previously, text messaging fees will apply to Twitter messages sent from and received by your phone. Also, setting up your phone on Twitter will allow you to send tweets out, but you don't necessarily have to receive other people's tweets on your phone. For now, however, check the box. The next section will show you how to alter the updates you receive,

or to stop them all together. Once you've checked the box, click on the "Save" button.

5. Now, wait for Twitter to send a text message to your phone. Within the text message will be a code, depending on where you live:

- United States: 0404
- Canada: 21212
- UK Short Code: 86444
- New Zealand Short Code: 8987
- Germany: +49 17 6888 50505
- Sweden: +46 737 494222
- India: 556651
- All Other: +44 762 4801423

If the numbers outside of the U.S. don't work, use the "All Other" number.

6. If you want to receive all of the updates from everyone you're following, you're set. If you don't, text the word "Off" to the applicable Twitter number from above.

Even if you plan on only using your cellphone for sending updates, you're still going to want to understand what each text command does.

Using designated Twitter text commands will help you get the best use out of your mobile device. You can use these commands from your phone, desktop, or the Web. To use them from your phone, just type in the command and send it to your country's Twitter number.

Twitter Text Commands Table

COMMAND / Function

ON. Turns all phone notifications on.

OFF. Turns all phone notifications off. You'll still receive notifications on the Web.

STOP (or QUIT). Stops all messages to your phone immediately. You'll still receive messages on the Web.

ON Username. Turns on notifications for a specific person on your phone. Example: **on TwiExample.**

OFF Username. Turns off notifications for a specific person on your phone. Example: **off TwiExample.**

FOLLOW Username. Allows you to start receiving notifications for a specific person on your phone. Functions the same as the "ON" command, plus allows you to start following someone new. Example: **follow TwiExample.**

LEAVE Username. Stops notifications from a specific person on your phone, without "unfollowing" the person. Functions the same as the "OFF" command. Example: **leave TwiExample.**

@username + message. Directs a tweet to another person and causes your tweet to save in their "replies" tab. Example: **@TwiExample Loved that article! Thanx for the link.**

D username + message. Sends a person a direct, private message that goes to their device and saves in their Web archive. Example: **D TwiExample Want to guest on my blog next week?**

WHOIS username. Retrieves profile information for any public user on Twitter. Example: **whois TwiExample.**

GET username. Retrieves the latest Twitter update posted by this person. Example: **get TwiExample.**

NUDGE username. Reminds a friend to update by asking what they're doing. Example: **nudge TwiExample.**

FAV username. Marks a specific person's tweet as a favorite. Example: **fav TwiExample.**

STATS. This command will display your number of followers, how many folks you're following, and your bio information. Example: **stats.**

INVITE phone number. This command sends an SMS Twitter invite to a real-life friend's mobile phone. Example: **Invite 555 555 5555.**

Try some of these commands, and see which ones most enhance your Twitter experience.

Top 10 mobile Twitter applications

Plenty of free and fee-based applications are available to even further customize your Twitter phone experience. Most of the free programs support these basic features:

- Support for multiple Twitter accounts.
- Auto refresh at user-defined intervals.
- Indicates the number of unread tweets.
- Tweets can be deleted quickly and easily.
- Can auto show / hide when new tweets arrive.
- Control over window layering and priority.
- Single-click access to user profile pages.
- Switches easily between friend and public tweets.
- Audio notification for new tweets.
- Ability to mark favorite tweets

These are the most popular applications, separated by device type:

Apple iPhone devices

Tweetdeck (http://tweetdeck.com)
If you use Tweetdeck on your PC or Mac, you'll probably like this iPhone version, which is also free.

Twitterific (http://iconfactory.com/software/twitterrific)
Twitterific is easily one of the most established mobile Twitter applications for the iPhone. You can try an ad-supported version for free, or you can pay $14.95 for an ad-free version.

Twitterfon (http://twitterfon.net)
Another popular application, Twitterfon offers a clean, easy-to-use interface. The paid version (Twitterfon Pro) costs $4.99,

and a free version also is available. Here is how Twitterfon describes the offerings of each version:

Tweetie (http://atebits.com/tweetie-iphone)
Tweetie does not offer a free version, though the cost is minimal at $2.99 from the App Store. Tweetie has an impressive list of features, fast response, and a built-in mini-browser.

Twitterlator (http://stone.com/twittelator)
Twitterlator offers a decent range of features in the free version, and the $4.99 Pro version is feature-packed.

Twikini (http://trinketsoftware.com/twikini/download.aspx)
Twikini is the only application in the top 10 for Windows Mobile devices. It's touted as offering a powerful and simple way for folks to use Twitter on their phone, and has a large array of features.

You can download Twikini for a free 14-day trial. If you decide you like it, you have several options for getting the full version. If you purchase another software application from the same company, they'll give you a 50 percent discount, which results in an end fee of $4.95. But if you have a blog or Web site and feel like posting something about Twikini, they'll give you the application for free. Or, you can choose the business version for $9.95. Of course, all of these prices could change at any time.

Nokia Series S60 devices

Gravity (http://mobileways.de/products/gravity/gravity)
Gravity is one of the few Twitter applications available for Nokia phones, and it is by far the most popular. You can download a free trial version; the full version costs anywhere from $9.95 to $34.95 depending on your phone and the services you want.

The features Gravity offers include:

- Compatibility with Twitter and Laconica.
- All functions available on your S60 phone: tweet, reply, DM, follow and unfollow, create favorites search, auto-update, and more.

- A tabbed view of your timeline, replies, messages, and friends.
- Configurable audio alerts for timeline, replies, DMs, and searches.
- Set up and use as many accounts as you want at the same time.
- Group support for creating custom tabs with user-defined filters.
- Twitter search section with multiple search and Twitter trends.
- Ability to post pictures to MobyPicture, Twitpic, TwitGoo, and Posterous.
- Ability to preview pictures from MobyPicture, Twitpic, or TwitGoo.
- Opening URLS from any tweet.
- Kinetic scrolling on S60v5 (Nokia 5800 and Nokia N97.)
- Theme support on S60v3.
- Full Screen mode on S60v3.
- Built-in auto update function and beta access for testing the latest features.

Blackberry devices

TwitterBerry (http://orangatame.com/products/twitterberry)

The Blackberry has very little to offer in the way of Twitter applications other than TwitterBerry. TwitterBerry works with more Blackberry models than any of the other applications available. Therefore, if TwitterBerry doesn't do what you want, do a quick search on "Twitter applications for Blackberry" and see whether any of the other offerings will work for your particular device.

TwitterBerry is a fairly basic application; however, it will make twittering by phone easier. It works over the data network and not through text messaging. The full application is free.

Cross-platform applications

Slandr (http://brothersoft.com/mobile/slandr-mobile-twitter-10670.html)

This cross platform works on Android, Blackberry, Java, Symbian, and Windows Mobile. It's also a Web-based application. Slandr uses Twitter's API, but delivers an enhanced mobile site for users. The interface is clean, attractive, and easy to navigate. It's free, but it's an ad-based application.

Some of Slandr's features are:

- Direct messaging, replies, and a public timeline.
- User and other searches.
- Mapping your friends.
- Twitterlocal integration.
- Favorites.

TinyTwitter (http://tinytwitter.com)

TinyTwitter is available for Java-enabled phones, such as Nokia and Blackberry, as well as for Windows Mobile devices, including Windows Pocket PC and Smartphone. Some of TinyTwitter's features include:

- Reply and direct message from the menu button.
- Audio alert when a new message arrives.
- The ability to set a time interval for checking new tweets.

If most of your Twitter time will be spent on your cellphone, then having the extra features an application offers should make your Twitter experience easier, more flexible, and probably a lot more fun. If, however, you only plan to use your phone for Twitter casually or sporadically, then you probably don't need to download an application.

Legally tweeting

Here's the legal stuff. Because local laws can vary, the principles here are basic. So, here's a guideline of some of the areas to tread carefully so you don't take unnecessary legal risks.

Defamation

Defamation covers both libelous activities (harming a person's reputation in writing), and slanderous activities (harming a person's reputation with the spoken word), which might apply to Twitter.

Language is considered defamatory if it harms the reputation of another person or company, whether it's direct, innuendo, satire, or implied, by you or someone else on Twitter. This isn't a new concept for business marketers who are careful about what they say in public forums.

Negligence

Negligence is the failure to exercise the degree of care the law requires for the protection of other persons. For example, let's imagine you're a psychiatrist, and you tweet about one of your patients. If you were to break patient/doctor confidentially by tweeting about your patient—and this had a negative effect and caused your patient mental anguish—your behavior could be considered negligence.

Trademark

Trademark law protects the investment in a particular brand. The protection might cover a company, like IBM, a celebrity whose name (while not trademarked) is their brand, or even a product, like Coca-Cola. To avoid running afoul of trademark law, don't use someone else's brand as your Twitter name, or give a false impression that you represent the company.

Privacy

Privacy is a personal right. Adhering to privacy law means you shouldn't disclose any information on Twitter that a "reasonable person" wouldn't want disclosed. You can't misrepresent someone's views, and you can't tweet that so-and-so did something they didn't do. Don't give out private information and don't lie about other people's views or actions.

Contracts

Tweeting is a form of publishing. Be careful not to "joke" on Twitter in a way that might be construed as promising a payment or service, otherwise you've entered into a contract.

Copyright

Is it possible to violate copyright in only 140 character? Sure. Think about it when you tweet song lyrics, quotes, or lines from poems.

Looking ahead

At the end of the day, Twitter should be fun. Take your first weeks somewhat slowly, learn everything you can about how Twitter works, become comfortable with tweeting and following. Then jump in and begin building your network, expanding your brand, and establishing yourself as an expert.

Even then, it should still be fun. The day Twitter begins to feel tedious and boring is the day you're doing something wrong. If that happens, take a step back and reassess your goals and your strategy. Somewhere, you took a misstep. Find it, fix it, and start again to master the world of conversing in 140 characters.

At the time of this writing, Twitter remains a free service that anyone with a cellphone or an Internet connection can join. While there are no guarantees of what will happen in the future, chances are that Twitter will eventually have to find a way to become profitable. A few possibilities include:

- Introducing paid services that replicate or expand on existing third-party applications. They'd have a market for them, especially those that require a user to submit their Twitter username and password in order to take advantage of the application. Many users would feel more comfortable paying a nominal fee for the same service through Twitter, and keeping their password 100 percent secure.
- Introducing entirely new services that would come with a one-time fee or a monthly charge.
- Introducing different levels of accounts, ranging from a free version that might only allow a certain number of tweets in a day, to higher increments of tweets, and possibly additional services for power tweeters, business tweeters, and others.
- Introducing its own fee-based background templates or custom design service.

If and when Twitter begins to charge for certain types of services, Twitter users will have some choices to make. Other microblogging platforms are out there, and there will always be a multitude of free applications for Twitter, so the future Twitter could be far different:

- Twitter could see an exodus of folks moving to a completely no-cost platform. While it's doubtful enough people would leave to tremendously hurt Twitter, stranger things have happened.
- Low-cost and free third-party Twitter applications will be in even more demand, especially those that don't require password information. People creative and skilled enough to create new applications using Twitter's API could find a new way to earn money.
- With the powerhouse Google running Jaiku, and the fact that many people are already using Plurk, Twitter could begin to lose a little of its shine.

Recommended reading

If you want to learn more about Twitter, there are tons of other books on the topic. Many focus on one specific area of Twitter use. For sources of current information, consult the list of blogs.

Books

- *Twitter Power: How to Dominate Your Market One Tweet at a Time.* **Joel Comm.**
- *The Twitter Book.* **Tim O'Reilly, Sarah Milstein.**
- *Twitter Tips, Tricks, and Tweets.* **Paul McFedries.**
- *Twitter For Dummies.* **Laura Fitton, Michael Gruen, and Leslie Poston.**
- *Twitter Revolution: How Social Media and Mobile Marketing is Changing the Way We Do Business & Market Online.* **Warren Whitlock , Deborah Micek.**
- *Twitter means business: how microblogging can help or hurt your company.* **Julio Ojeda-Zapata**
- *All a Twitter: A Personal and Professional Guide to Social Networking with Twitter.* **Tee Morris.**

Blogs

- **Official Twitter Blog.**: http://blog.twitter.com

- **TwiTip.** Using Twitter for business. http://twitip.com
- **Twittercism.** Tools, hints, tricks and opinions. http://twittercism.com
- **Twitterrati.** The world of Twitter and microblogging. http://twitterrati.com

Index

Alphabetical Index

LaVergne, TN USA
05 October 2009
159849LV00005B/35/P

9 780977 240661